The Cumberland Association

Celebrating 175 Years of Leadership, Ministry and Service

Roy W. Harris
Phillip T. Morgan

Copyright 2018

By

Dr. Roy W. Harris

ISBN 978-1947759046

Soft cover

All rights reserved
No part of this book may be reproduced or transmitted in any form or by any means, electronic or mechanical, including photocopying, recording, or by any information storage and retrieval system, without permission in writing from the copyright owner.

This book was printed in the United States of America.

To order additional copies of this book:

Order Online
@
www.amazon.com

Contents

Introduction – 5

Founding of the Cumberland Association – 9

Interesting Events, People, Places and Things – 29

Names of the Cumberland Association – 43

Moderators, Clerks and General Information 45

Quarterly Meetings of the Cumberland Association – 77

Churches and Pastors – 83

Fulfilling the Great Commission – 89

Advocates for Education – 97

The Women of the Cumberland – 109

Publications, Literature and Reading Materials – 125

Opposition to Alcohol – 129

Communication with Outside Organizations – 133

General Conference of Free Will Baptists – 137

National Association of Free Will Baptists – 141

Tennessee State Association of Free Will Baptists – 147

Free Will Baptist Home for Children – 151

174th Cumberland Association Meeting Minutes – 157

Introduction

By

Roy W. Harris

1843 marked the halfway point of tenth president of the United States John Tyler's term and there were 26 states in the Union. Robert E. Lee was the Post Engineer at Fort Hamilton in Brooklyn, N.Y., and a member of West Point's board of visitors. Ulysses S. Grant graduated 21st in a class of 39 from the United States Military Academy at West Point and Charles Dickens published his now famous story, *A Christmas Carol*.

October 1843 is important for another reason. It marked the beginning of a long and rich history for Free Will Baptists in middle Tennessee with the birth of the Cumberland Association of Free Will Baptists at *Heads Meeting House* in Robertson County. *Elder William Barton* delivered the sermon from Acts 10:34-35. William Barton was elected moderator and *Wilson L. Gower* was elected clerk. The offering for the day was $7.32 ($206 in today's money.)

The Cumberland Association has impacted Free Will Baptists on local, state and national levels in a variety of ways. The Association was a force for higher Christian education and at the forefront of the dream and later reality of Free Will Baptist Bible College, now Welch College.

Its churches have been a strong underpinning of support for North American Missions, International Missions and all National Association of Free Will Baptists' ministries throughout its 175 year history.

The Cumberland has also been a strong believer and participant in the Tennessee Free Will Baptist State work from the beginning and continues to rigorously support the Tennessee Free Will Baptist State Office.

The following pages were written to celebrate the rich heritage and history of the Cumberland Association of Free Will Baptists. Our goal in writing the book was to highlight achievements, individuals, institutions, and a variety of things that should be remembered.

This book was not designed to provide an exhaustive study or a year-by-year account of the activities and accomplishments of the Cumberland Association.

Detailed research was conducted using historical documents housed in the Free Will Baptist Historical Collection in the library of Welch College in Gallatin, Tennessee. 175 years of annual association minutes were reviewed, analyzed and important details were noted.

We endeavored to stay as true as possible to the actual wording of the minutes. Individual names, community locations, church names, grammar and etc. were written exactly as they appeared in the minutes.

A copy of the 2017 published minutes, minus individuals contact information, completes the final chapter of the book.

Other documents were also reviewed in preparation for this book.

A brief account of Free Will Baptist history in middle Tennessee, prior to the formation of the Cumberland Association in 1843, is also included in the book. There are more exhaustive historical records available in other books and publications.

Writing a book such as this is a daunting task. No doubt there will be individuals, incidences and activities that some might feel should have been included. We wish we could have included everyone who contributed to and made a difference in serving through the Cumberland Association and other events but that would have been an impossible task.

The book doesn't examine detailed histories of organizations the Cumberland had interaction with. Other outside resources are available and suggested throughout the book.

We pray that this book will serve as a reminder of the Cumberland Association's valued contribution to Christ and His kingdom, to Tennessee Free Will Baptists and to Free Will Baptists across America and around the world.

We are hopeful that the book will also be remembered by future generations of Free Will Baptists as a historical document written in 2018, which reviewed and celebrated 175 years of Cumberland Association history.

Founding of the Cumberland Association

By
Phillip T. Morgan

The Cumberland Association of Free Will Baptists was founded in 1843. Most of the folks who gathered that day to hold the first business session and hear the sermons were the children of the frontier. Their parents or grandparents had moved to the region with the first parties of settlers. Probably they did not realize how much sacrificial labor had been given in order to bring them together that day and certainly they could have no idea what God was going to do in the future through their faithful obedience.

Unfortunately, the same could be said for most of us. The regular cycle of associational meetings wind on and we often take for granted all they portend. The Cumberland Association not only provides our churches with accountability and fellowship, it is the vessel of our collective memory. Through our regular associational relationship we bear witness to the activity of God beyond our individual churches. More, if we cast our eye back we can discern even grander vistas of God's providence inscribed not in moments but generations or even centuries.

This chapter is an introduction into God's marvelous work through our forbearers in the Cumberland Association of Free Will Baptists. Over the past thirty years, Robert

Picirilli, more than anyone, has worked to uncover our past so that we might appreciate the sacrifice that made our present possible. What follows is in some ways a condensation of his work on Robert Heaton's ministerial record book, which can be found in *Little Known Chapters in Free Will Baptist History* (Randall House, 2015). However, several new items of interest are also included. Certain aspects of Heaton's record that Picirilli mentions in passing are given more detail and various new interpretations are offered for consideration.[1] Hopefully, this will encourage us all to engage our heritage faithfully and prepare for our future intentionally.

Migration into the Backcountry

Settlers began making homes on the banks of the Cumberland River in the late eighteenth century. Families from Virginia, North Carolina, Canada and Europe walked or floated on canoes from the Appalachian Mountains in order to find a better life in the thick dark forests that spread out from the river's banks. They were pioneers in every sense of the word. Hardy. Determined. Adventurous. Industrious. Full of faith in God's providence, they made the long and difficult journey.

Many were killed brutally during Indian attacks spurred on by the Spanish. More died of disease. But those who lived began clearing forests so they could scrape a livelihood from the rocky soil. For their food and that of their livestock, they planted corn, turnips, potatoes, squash, peas, beans, wheat and oats. Some of their fields

---

[1] Interpretations that differ from Picirilli's have not been offered lightly, for in all of these matters he has been the trailblazer and he deserves our deepest gratitude. Where he has cleared forests, I am cleaning out some of

were used to raise tobacco for personal use and to make a small profit. In those early years, there were less than a thousand American settlers in the entire Middle Tennessee area.

      Much of this migration was sponsored by the work of a land speculator named Judge Henderson who worked for the Transylvania Company. Having come to loggerheads with the state of Virginia about the bluegrass frontier land that would eventually become Kentucky, Henderson set his sights on the Cumberland Basin because it lay within the bounds of Washington County, North Carolina. Henderson hired James Robertson to lead the settlement, but in the end, two groups comprised the settlement. Robertson led a group of men over land through the Cumberland Gap and across Kentucky then down to the Cumberland River while John Donelson led the second group that included the women and children by river on a "flotilla of flatboats."[i] Among the men and women that survived the dangerous trek were the forbearers of the Cumberland Association of Free Will Baptists.

Robert Heaton's Early Ministry

      Amos and Elizabeth (d. 1815) Heaton actually arrived in the Cumberland basin with their family just prior to the Robertson Party. This makes the Heatons some of the earliest settlers in Middle Tennessee. Indeed, the Robertson and Heaton parties must have nearly arrived on the same day.[ii] For this reason some historians have thought that the Heatons and Robertsons were part of the same party. While they did travel in separate groups, the two families were very familiar with each other and had been neighbors back in Virginia. Further, many of the families that arrived during those early years were related in one way or another.[iii]

When the Heatons first decided to move to the frontier they settled on the Holton River near modern day Kingsport, Tennessee. At the time, this piece of land was also part of the Virginia colony. After the War for Independence, they continued moving with the frontier. On December 24, 1779, they settled just north of the Cumberland River on the outskirts of modern day Davidson County. Amos and Elizabeth's first child was named Robert (1765-1843).

Robert was a part of his family's migration westward and likely helped drive the livestock and hunt for supper along the way. Once they reached their destination, fourteen-year-old Robert would have played an important part in raising a cabin, clearing trees and plowing behind the mules. We know very little about other aspects of his early life. Yet sometime over the next twenty years, he came to saving faith in Christ and was baptized. Where he heard the gospel and who baptized him remains unknown.

After reaching adulthood, Robert married a woman named Elisabeth (a.1764-1837) and together they had five children (three girls and two boys). During their life together, he amassed a large landholding through inheritance and acquisition. Several slaves helped him work this land, probably raising corn, wheat and tobacco. Obviously, Heaton was quite a wealthy man and a shrewd in his business dealings.

At age forty-four, something significant changed in Heaton's life. On August 22, 1809, he preached his first sermon. Whatever prompted this change wasn't fleeting, because after three years of preparation he was ordained to the gospel ministry on May 10, 1812. Unfortunately, we have no information about who ordained him or instructed him in his Arminian Baptistic doctrine.

Perhaps there were people with ties to the Paul Palmer Movement of Free Will Baptists in the Carolinas. Some early histories have claimed that Free Will Baptists were in the Turnersville area of Robertson County as early as 1798 when supposedly Nathan Arnett and Jonathan Darden "gathered members of that denomination into a church" that later lapsed.[iv] This assertion hasn't been corroborated, but neither has it been disproven. So perhaps there were remnants from that early church who had ties to the Palmer Movement who instructed Heaton, set him aside for the ministry and filled his first church. Regardless, Heaton's ministry saw immediate success and by the end of the year, he had baptized or "received" twenty-four people, including his younger brother Enoch.

As Picirilli has noted, there is some evidence that there were multiple large revival meetings during the years 1811 and 1812. These revivals and others like them might have instigated Heaton's call to the ministry as well as provided a context for his early success. But it is also true that the expanded religious liberty of the frontier in connection with America's independence led to steady growth among Baptists throughout the young nation.[v]

The details about these earliest years of Heaton's ministry are scant, but it seems that he began his ministry in 1812 by reorganizing a defunct church in the White's Creek area named Zion Church. The following year Benjamin Drake and William Cradock became the first deacons of this reorganized group of believers and Heaton's newly baptized brother, Thomas, began serving as the clerk.[vi] Heaton continued to build up this church for the next eleven years.

Heaton, like almost all Baptist ministers of the day,

would have preached in a frontier vernacular that he shared with the common folks around him. Through direct and clear presentations of the gospel, many common frontier folk came to saving faith.[vii] Each year, he baptized and received a few people and some were lost through death, transfer or dismissal. Still, the growth continued, and by 1823, Zion Church was reporting 114 members in good standing.

Like John Bunyan's pilgrim, Christian, following Christ must have made Heaton seem odd to his wife and children. For ten years he preached and ministered in the surrounding countryside before his wife and children came to faith. Thankfully, in 1822 his faithful witness was rewarded as Elisabeth and four of their five children came to faith and were baptized.

Ministering to Slaves

Another important aspect of Heaton's work was his ministry among slaves. During the first half of the nineteenth century, Baptists and Methodists were about the only Christians trying to reach enslaved people.[viii] Many Baptist churches in the south prior to the War Between the States included both black and white members.[ix] By the 1830s, it became common practice to relegate the black members to the back pews, but not in every instance.[x] While we don't know the seating arrangement in Heaton's churches, his black congregants seem to have appreciated their relationship with him.

Throughout his record, Heaton mentions at least thirteen black men and women who were part of his ministry.[xi] Most of them are described as "servants" but not all, making it possible that at least some of them were free. Slave owners at the turn of the eighteenth century held various positions regarding the faith of their slaves. Some encouraged or forced their slaves to attend church and earnestly sought their conversion, whereas others forbade their slaves from even attending churches. Still others were ambivalent about the issue and allowed their slaves limited freedom in this regard.[xii]

For his part, Heaton seems to have allowed his slaves to determine their own spiritual course. Of the people we know he owned, only one of them, Jenny, could possibly be present in his record.[xiii] But Heaton was not unconcerned about the souls of slaves. Rather, he was actively involved in winning them to Christ, since he baptized almost all thirteen black people included in his book. Neither were they forced to join his church by their owners. Almost none of them attended the same church as the people who owned them. In fact, one slave named Dicey might have been actively involved in leading the Vick family that owned him to Christ. Heaton baptized Dicey in September 1816. Nearly a year later four members of the Vick family followed Dicey's example and were baptized.

Each of these men and women was also invited to join Heaton's churches. When Heaton reported numbers of members to various associations, the slaves recorded in his register were included in the total. In addition, one married couple named Sam and Elsabeth, who were "servants of Mr. Criddle," were received by letter in 1821. This act of church government highlights their official status as members in the church. Most likely, as members, the black congregants celebrated the Lord's Supper and practiced feet washing with their white counterparts.

Obviously, the specific details of how black and white congregants related to one another remain unknown. However, there is evidence that the black congregants appreciated Heaton's ministry above others. When he began a new work in 1832, five of the black members of his earlier churches seem to have moved their membership to be with him. In the end, the black congregants of these churches and the ones that would follow probably separated from their white brothers and sisters after emancipation as they did in the Cape Fear Conference of Free Will Baptists in North Carolina.

Growing Ministry

After seven years building up Zion Church, Heaton began branching out. During 1819, he began a new work on Sycamore Creek in Robertson County that was connected with his work at Zion. Three years after starting his work along Sycamore Creek, Heaton decided it was time to separate the Sweet Spring Church on Sycamore Creek, as it was called by that time, from the Zion Church. Perhaps he made this decision because of his confidence in a new member of his church, John M. Chaudoin.

Chaudoin and his wife Sarah were received by letter as members of Zion Church in 1822. He might have already been ordained, since Heaton quickly put him in a place of leadership. From 1822 to 1826, Heaton led the development of the Sweet Spring Church while Chaudoin led Zion. At least two other Baptistic churches were also active in the area at this time, Liberty and McAdoo Creek. These churches were associated with Separate Baptist organizations in Kentucky and probably carried on friendly relations with Zion and Sweet Spring.

Sometime between 1813 and 1815, Heaton also began building relationships with Separate Baptists in Kentucky. This indicates that Heaton at least had common cause with Separate Baptists who were accepting of

Arminian theology and practiced open communion, believer's baptism and feet washing.[xiv] However, Heaton didn't actually refer to any of his churches as "Separate Baptist" until 1839. Such ambiguity might mean little, but it could also suggest that Heaton didn't precisely think of himself as a Separate Baptist. Perhaps living on the sparsely settled frontier, Heaton simply chose to seek mutual support from the only nearby Arminian Christians who weren't Methodists.

Regardless of his reasons, joining in association with other churches seems to have been important to Heaton. He represented Zion Church at the South Kentucky Association of Separate Baptists until it split amiably in 1819. When this organization decided to divide, Heaton led the Zion church to join the southernmost division named the Nolin Association where he remained an active member for the next ten years.[xv]

In 1821, Heaton helped write the annual circular letter for the churches in the Nolin Association. These letters were used to promote right doctrine and combat false doctrine. In his letter, Heaton emphasized adherence to God's word as the only rule for faith and practice. He also exhorted the readers to do everything in love. In later statements, Heaton went further by rejecting "all human rules or articles of faith or decorems."[xvi] Rejecting formal statements of faith was common on the frontier at the time, but Heaton's churches would abandon this position during the next fifty years.

Despite his involvement in the Nolin Association, around 1830 Heaton seems to have grown dissatisfied, making his last appearance three years later. His reasons for leaving the association are not certain, but the contentious years of 1826 through 1828 might have played a part. During these years, Heaton and Chaudoin were engaged in a strong disagreement of some sort that led to the breaking of their fellowship in a very public manner. Most likely, the disagreement stemmed from Heaton's attempts to establish a new church.

Troubled Times

For unknown reasons, Heaton decided to gather a new church in 1826 originally named Marrowbone Church and later Charity Church. Despite its eventual name, the church's founding seems to have been greeted with little love. Heaton provides a list of members for this new church, which, as Picirilli has shown, consisted almost completely of former members of Zion and Sweet Spring.[xvii] At first, Chaudoin seems to have raised no objection to this. Instead, he is reported as giving the "hand of friendship" to Heaton at the forming of the new church.[xviii] But Chaudoin either changed his mind or secretly harbored animosity toward Heaton.

The ensuing fall-out spilled over into the Nolin Association. Chaudoin petitioned the association not to admit the new church at the 1826 meeting held at Zion's meeting house. A committee was appointed to examine the matter. After hearing the report of Chaudoin and his witnesses, the committee concluded that there wasn't sufficient reason to bar Marrowbone Church from joining the association.[xix] However, Chaudoin refused to accept the findings of the committee.

Over the next year, Chaudoin seems to have led Zion, Sweet Spring and Liberty Church in an attack against Heaton and Marrowbone Church. They sent out letters of opposition against the new church and Chaudoin openly declared that he wouldn't listen to the association. Such behavior wasn't received well by the members of the Nolin, who declared Chaudoin and any churches associated with him out of fellowship in 1827.[xx] At this point Chaudoin made a last effort to defend himself by penning and publishing a venomous screed against Heaton and the Nolin Association that earned him only public ridicule and the revocation of his credentials.[xxi]

Heaton was publically vindicated and even preached at the next association meeting, but much damage had been done. The Zion, Sweet Spring and Liberty Churches no longer reported to the Nolin and probably disbanded soon thereafter. The Marrowbone Church also declined in membership over this time. Despite the vindication of the Nolin, Heaton's interest in the association seems to have flagged. After 1828, he only reported to the association twice more, in 1830 and 1833. After that, Heaton spent six years outside any formal association, working with the small but growing number of churches in his area.

Wilson L. Gower

The recovery of Heaton's work was led, in part, by Wilson L. Gower (1793-1865). He was also related to the first settlers of Middle Tennessee. The Gower family emigrated from England during the eighteenth century, settling for a time in North Carolina. However, they quickly began moving further inland and Wilson's grandfather Abel Gower (1725-1780) joined the Robertson Party as they left to settle the Cumberland.[xxii] In fact, the Gowers and Robertsons might have been related through marriage.[xxiii] Three of Abel Gower's five sons made professions of faith and joined the Methodist church in 1801. A year later, all three began preaching. One of the three, Russell, served as a Methodist Minister until 1831 and was Wilson's father.[xxiv]

There is very little information about Wilson Gower before he met Heaton. From what little evidence there is, it appears that Gower married Charlotte Baird in 1812.[xxv] Charlotte died soon thereafter and though the cause of death is unknown, complications during childbirth commonly killed women in the nineteenth century. Gower remarried in 1820 to a woman in Heaton's church, Lucindy Page. Page had been baptized by Heaton the year before and perhaps she was influential in leading her new husband to Christ.[xxvi] After two years of marriage, in 1822, Gower was also baptized by Heaton and the new couple became active members of the church. When Heaton started the Marrowbone Church in 1826, the Gowers followed him with Wilson serving as the clerk. They also remained faithful throughout the Chaudoin controversy and the difficult years that followed.

However, in 1832 the Gowers were dismissed by letter so they could begin working to gather more churches. Gower was a "mighty man in the Scriptures in his day." Like most Free Will Baptists of the time, he had limited access to education, but he was "very well trained theologically" and reputedly "possessed large common sense, and sound piety, good judgement, and a burning zeal for the salvation of souls."[xxvii] Though Gower was preaching on the frontier during the height of the Second Great Awakening's evangelistic fervor, he did not neglect to take seriously God's call to "promote" His kingdom in the earth.[xxviii] His attention to the present can be seen in his diligent work building relationships and associations between churches.

Soon after leaving Marrowbone Church, the Gowers gathered Blue Spring Church in what most likely is modern day northern Davidson County. Heaton and Gower remained close and their relationship seems to have underpinned a growing sense of sisterly association between their churches. In 1833, they attended the Nolin Association for the last time, likely in order to make a final decision about continuing with the organization.[xxix] They apparently decided to withdraw, although we don't know why.

The Concord Association and New Churches

After leaving the Nolin, Marrowbone Church (now called Charity) and Blue Spring Church seem to have associated with each other exclusively for the next four years. Then in 1837, Gower led Blue Spring to join the Concord Association of Separate Baptists #2. That year, both he and Heaton preached for the association. However, Heaton did not lead Charity Church to join until the following year.[xxx] The Concord Association #2 was organized as a distinct group of Arminian Baptists in Tennessee around 1826 or 1827. Prior to that time, they had been joined with Calvinist Baptists in an association known as the Concord Association, but apparently their theological differences led them to go their separate ways.

Interestingly, Heaton first refers to his church as the "Church of Christ called Separate Baptist" at this time. There is no doubt that the name Church of Christ had no connection to the work of Alexander Campbell, since many non-Campbellite churches incorporated versions of this title at the time.[xxxi] As Picirilli has concluded, adopting the title "Separate Baptist" might mean little since Heaton had been associating with Separate Baptists for nearly twenty-five years by this time.[xxxii] But this change could also reflect Heaton's thinking about the importance of associations. After five years of virtual isolation, Heaton chose to join another Separate Baptist association. Adopting the name might have be an attempt to solidify his commitment (even if only for his own benefit) to this organization. To say, "If we're going to do this, let's do it with all our might." Whatever his reasons for adopting the name, Heaton, along with Gower, remained an active member of the association until 1842.

During this time, several new churches were gathered within Heaton and Gower's circle of influence. In 1838, Heaton apparently tried unsuccessfully to revive the old Zion Church, which seems to have disbanded after Chaudoin's disgrace. Around the same time, Good Spring Church in Robertson County was gathered. Perhaps Gower and Heaton worked together toward this end, since they were both part of the presbytery called by the church in June 1838 to examine Thomas Felts for ordination. Felts served as the minister at Good Spring for a short while following his ordination. However, when he moved to Kentucky in 1840, Heaton took over and began ministering at both Marrowbone and Good Spring Church.[xxxiii]

Two of Heaton's protégés also were starting churches in the growing Cumberland area. Whether or not Arnette and Darden really did gather a Free Will Baptist church in Turnersville in the late eighteenth century, the current Heads Free Will Baptist Church was gathered in that community by 1840. George Head (1794-1868) who was baptized by Heaton in 1835, might have gathered this church on his own or he might have worked with Gower. He and Gower knew one another well and later Head gave his daughter Milly in marriage to Gower's son James.[xxxiv]

Regardless of whether they worked together, Head took his new faith seriously, at times allowing preachers to hold services in his home.[xxxv] He might also have been ordained to the gospel ministry.[xxxvi] Even if he wasn't ordained, on the frontier Baptists commonly gave lay leaders some pastoral responsibilities out of necessity.[xxxvii] By 1840, he was actively involved in the leadership of Heads Church, representing the congregation at the Concord Association #2 along with Charles Lankford. This church is the oldest continuously meeting church in what would become the Cumberland Association.

Whether or not Gower was active at Heads Church during this time, he began taking the gospel further west. By 1841, he had gathered a new church in Stewart County named Liberty Church.[xxxviii] This might have been a revival of the old Liberty Church that sided with Chaudoin in the 1820s, but it could also be a completely new congregation. Gower didn't allow this new work to detract from his responsibilities at Blue Spring however. He continued to lead both of these congregations for several years.

A sixth church came under Heaton's circle of influence at this time. Mount Zion Church in Tennessee began reporting to the Concord Association #2 in 1841. R. R. and William Barton represented the congregation at this meeting, but who they were or where they or Mount Zion Church came from is unknown. Regardless of their previous knowledge of one another, Mount Zion Church began building relationships with the Heaton, Gower and Head churches. The growing bond between these churches was highlighted in 1842 when they decided to form their own association.

The divided organizations of the original Concord Association had remained friendly since their break in the late 1820s. The Arminian Concord Association #2 and Calvinist Concord Association #1 began considering reunification around 1840. As this possibility became more likely, the Heaton, Gower, Head and Barton churches were faced with a difficult decision. When the Concord Association #2 voted in 1842 to reunite with the Concord Association #1, the churches of the Cumberland basin decided to withdraw. As Picirilli has argued, it seems that their Arminian theology commitment was too strong to join in communion with the Calvinists.[xxxix] The next year they founded their own association named the Cumberland Association of Separate Baptists.

Present at the Creation

On Saturday, September 30, 1843, families of believers from Davidson, Robertson and Stewart Counties (including the area that would one day become Cheatham County) began to converge on the small wooded dell in Turnersville where Heads Church had their meetinghouse. With most of the crops already in the barn for the year, they left their fields and kitchens to rest as they walked, rode horses and packed people into wagons to make the trip. The baskets hanging from their arms bulged with bread, cured meats, roasted vegetables, fresh butter and jars of fruit preserves and fresh honey. No doubt, they met up with old friends as they made their way along the cow paths and wagon roads that led to their destination. Perhaps they sang the old hymns of the faith as they traveled and talked of the power of Christ's blood.

Robert Heaton, now seventy-eight years old, full of years and only a month away from his eternal reward, was part of the growing throng. What must he have thought as he watched the sheaves of his labor being brought in? To see Gower in the midst of a group from Stewart County and Head inviting folks to tie up their horses around back in the shade near the water. As baskets of food for supper were unloaded and brothers and sisters in Christ began to mingle, did he think of his first sermon under the shifting shade of the trees so long ago? Did he reminisce on all the cold baptisms in little creeks and ponds dappling the rolling countryside? Was his joy invested with a rich sorrow by Elisabeth's absence (she had died six years earlier)? Perhaps he paused to ponder the sovereignty of God in the miscues with Chaudoin or the churches that had been lost. Did his heart brim and then overflow with the savory sweetness of God's unmerited favor toward him? Surely so.

That afternoon William Barton, the most recent addition to the group of ministers, stood before the congregation and preached from Acts 10:34-35 calling them to fear God and work righteousness that they might enjoy God's approval. After the sermon, the association sat for its first business session. Sycamore Church represented by William Railey, John Wingo and Thomas Smith was received into the organization that already included Blue Spring, Charity, Good Spring, Heads, Liberty and Mount Zion. Barton was elected moderator and Gower clerk. A committee was appointed to arrange the services for the following day and make logistical arrangements for the rest of the session.

After business was adjourned, many of the local homes would have been opened to house the guests who had traveled so far. Others would have slept under the cool Autumn stars. The next day, a Sunday, Gower, Barton and James M. Cherry from Liberty Church preached sermons to a "large and attentive congregation."[xl] Between the preaching sessions, the congregation would have enjoyed times of rural fellowship: comparing each farmer's tobacco crop for the year, discussing how best to mend a torn dress or keep rabbits out of the turnip patch and showing off new babies.

    The next morning at 9:00 the business resumed. A finance committee was appointed to steward the $7.32 offering given by the churches (a very good offering indeed considering the time and place it was given). After deciding to hold the next association meeting at Liberty Church the following year, they recommended that Barton and Gower prepare a circular letter to be distributed at that meeting. No doubt, this letter would be used to protect doctrinal purity as they had been in the Nolin Association. The church representatives also recommended that each church vote on a budget to financially support a travelling preacher and commit themselves to the budget by reporting the total to the Cumberland. This reflects the general practice of the time among Baptists for one minister to oversee multiple churches.[xli]

    Nearing the end of the meeting, they scheduled times for each church to observe the Lord's Supper when all ministers would endeavor to be present. After appointing B. F. Binkley to oversee the printing of three hundred copies of the minutes, Gower was asked to close the meeting in prayer. As clerk, Gower recorded that the meeting was closed in "much peace and great harmony." Folks began loading wagons and saying their long goodbyes. Traveling home, Heaton must have wondered what the future would hold and what kind of fruit these churches would bear after he was gone.

Conclusion

    The next thirty-three years span some of the most tumultuous years in America's history. Most of the crowd gathered under the shade of the trees that fateful day in 1843 would soon experience the ravages of war and the burden of occupation. Already the frontier had moved on into Texas, Arizona, Utah and Wyoming. These children of the pioneers would have to learn to live in a completely reordered society that embraced machines over people, factories over fields and cities over churches. Unfortunately, this entire experience remains a complete mystery to us.

The records of the Cumberland Association between 1843 and 1876 have been lost. Some might have been preserved and buried in a stack of microfilm in some archive, but they might have all been destroyed by the ravages of time and war. Some memories of these years survived and were recorded though, and other features can be deduced.

Gower's son James W. and Headsson George R. continued the legacy of their fathers, calling sinners to repentance and building Christ's kingdom on earth. To their number were added other ministers including two ministers named Rose and Stewart. Around the year 1851, the Cumberland Association added *Free Will* to their name becoming Free Will Separate Baptists. A few years after the war, they dropped *Separate* and became the Cumberland Association of Free Will Baptists.[xlii]

Perhaps more importantly, the Cumberland Association adopted a confession of faith and constitution during this interval. The statement of faith clearly but simply expressed their Reformed Arminian doctrine that honors the depravity of man as well as the general atonement while rejecting the doctrine of repeated regeneration. Feet washing was listed among the ordinances that all Christians have a duty to perform. Their church government was associational, but the association didn't have power to "lord it over God's heritage, nor to infringe upon the inherent rights of the churches." In short, they sounded very much like most Free Will Baptist churches that descended from Paul Palmer's work in North Carolina. Whether these documents reflect a codification of Heaton and Gower's doctrine or the influence of later Free Will Baptists from the Palmer Movement, we don't know.

During the twentieth century, the Cumberland Association would grow to one of the largest Free Will Baptist associations in the nation. The member churches and ministers of the Cumberland have played a significant role in the formation and leadership of the National Association of Free Will Baptists. The women of the association have also spread their influence far beyond the confines of the Cumberland Basin. After 175 years of faithful service, the Cumberland Association of Free Will Baptists is still striving to serve God faithfully in Middle Tennessee, the denomination and around the world. Let us take the heritage we have received as task.

Interesting Events, People, Places, and Things

By
Roy W. Harris

This chapter is filled with interesting things. Here is a sampling: the first lady elected to a position in the Cumberland Association, opposition to racetrack gambling in Tennessee, recommendation of a Cumberland minister to the Secretary of War in 1917 to serve as a chaplain in the United States Army, reference to a state law that required the public school principals to begin each day reading a portion of the Bible and more.

The sessions are listed in chronological order and span a variety of subjects. You will be surprised, amazed and maybe even shocked a little as you move through the years.

33rd session 1876 - *Reverend J.W. Gower appointed to write the history of the Free Will Baptists of Cumberland Association of Tennessee, and request any one that can give him any information to write and send it to Thomasville Post Office, TN.*

42nd session 1885 - *We find great want of system in Church government; therefore we would recommend that each Church have written in its Church books a Compact of Principles or Church Constitution.*

47th session 1890 - *We thank God for the increasing favor manifested by the brotherhood generally toward the union of all white Liberal Baptists of the South in one unitary and cooperative association.*

54th session 1897 - *Resolutions* first began to come into focus in 1897.

60th session 1903 - First mention of motions being made and passed.

62nd session 1905 – Voted to change meeting from 3 days down to 2 days.
First appearance of the *Government and Constitution* found in the minutes. *Articles of Faith* and *Rules of Decorum* had appeared in earlier minutes.

63rd session 1906 - *That we the members of the Freewill Baptist indorse the bill passed by the last Tennessee Legislature, called the Anti-racetrack gambling bill, that was declared unconstitutional, urge that it again be sustained by our representatives in a form that accords with the constitution.*

64th session - October 23-25, 1907 (back to 3 days)

66th session 1909 - *Resolved: Motion prevailed in which the <u>Gospel Voice Hymnal</u> was adopted as our standard song book, and recommended to be used by all the churches.*

68th session 1911 – Clerk Mrs. H.P. Smith - First Lady elected as an officer.

Resolved: Whereas we as Freewill Christian Baptist of the Cumberland Association have made mistakes in taking into our Presbytery as ministers, from other denominations who have done us much harm, and we therefore offer the following resolutions: Be it Resolved.
- *That we require all ministers coming from other denominations to come well recommended.*
- *That they be required to serve a probation of twelve months before they be admitted into our Presbytery as full fledge members of said Presbytery.*

71st session 1914 - *Resolved: That the time of the Association be changed to Wednesday before the fourth Sunday in October. The sermon to be preached at 11:00 a.m. at the next session.*

74th session 1917 - *We recommend Reverend Joe Gower to the Honorable Secretary of War for a Chaplaincy in the United States Army.*

Moderator is to appoint a committee to draw up a *code of laws* by which the Association shall be governed. Reverend J.L. Welch and Reverend J.E. Hudgins were appointed to draw up these laws.

Established that *each church in this Association shall be entitled to one vote and each church having more than fifty members shall have one vote for the first fifty and one vote for every additional fifty or fraction thereof.*

First Report: Ladies Aid Societies– Ladies Aid Society met at Oaklawn. *Mrs. Edgar Parker* – President, *Mrs. W. M White* Secretary. Total in treasury, $49.72 and also nine quilts on hand.

The ordaining council made some of its first recommendations to the Association. Two men were recommended and two more were required to devote themselves to the study of the Bible for another year.

75th session 1918 - Voted to seek membership in the General Assembly of Free Will Baptists.

78th session 1921 - The State Ladies Aid of the Free Will Baptist Church of Tennessee met at Bethlehem Church on September 28, 1921 and sent a report to the Cumberland Association Annual Meeting.
They also mentioned their desire to open an orphanage and establish a denomination school.

81st session 1924 – Association Dues - *The pastor of each church collect five dollars for their churches and funds to be brought to the treasurer of this Association.*

82nd session 1925 - The Association voted to: *purchase two hundred dollars stock in North Carolina Ayden Press. One hundred and eighty dollars were subscribed by public donation for this cause.*

Ladies Aid Societies of Free Will Baptists of Tennessee - 18 Societies have been formed, with six formed during this past year.

88th session 1931 - From the Education and Literature Committee: *We feel thankful to our law making bodies for so arranging school laws, that no school principal can legally teach without reading, or causing to be read, a portion of God's Word each day for our children.*

91ˢᵗ session 1934 –
- *Sister Fanny Polston spoke of the women's work through the General Conferences.*
- *Reverend Paul Woolsey brought a very interesting message from the Union Association of East Tennessee.*
- *Officer Terms – Officers to serve for two years (changed from one-year term.)*

92ⁿᵈ session 1935 – Women's Auxiliary – This was the first mention of the Women's Auxiliary in the Cumberland minutes. The Ladies Aid had been mentioned many times before.

96ᵗʰ session 1939 - *The History of the Cumberland Association as copied from the Free Will Baptist Encyclopedia at Mt. Zion Bible School, Blakely, Georgia, February 1939 by Huey Gower:*

The Cumberland Association of Free Will Christian Baptists is located in the northern part of the state, east of the Tennessee River. It was organized in 1842 by Elders Robert Eaton and W.M. Gower.

The Concord Association of Free Will Baptists was divided on the subject of Communion and the Liberty, Charity, Heads, Blue Springs and Sullivan Churches practicing open communion, withdrew to form this Association. It has continued its work with good success. The churches now (1888) number eighteen, as follows in the Dover quarterly meeting: Liberty, Spring Hill, Rock Springs, Pleasant Valley, Bethel, Collision's Chapel and Sinking Springs.

In the Ashland quarterly meeting: Good Springs, Heads, Bethlehem, Oakland, Charity, Zion, Oaklawn, and North Nashville.

99th session 1942 - Reverend Robert Crawford first mentioned as leading a song with Reverend Henry Melvin at the piano.

100th session 1943 - *J.E. Hudgens delivered message titled: One Hundred Years in Review. He told of bodies of the Cumberland Association dated as far back as 1809. Men and movements were spoken of such as Reverend Robert Heaton who called himself a Separate Baptist. Men came from other Associations such as the South Kentucky Association. These men and Associations merged to form the Cumberland Association of TN in 1843.*

102nd session 1945 – *Reverend Homer Willis brought a devotion in the Thursday morning session.*

106th session 1949 – *Reverend Charles Thigpen delivered the morning message from Jude 1:3 – Contend for the Faith That Was Once Delivered Unto the Saints.*

Resolution Passed

We discourage our people, especially our youth against the reading of Love Novels, True Story magazines, Murder Stories and books and like magazines. Also, that they not attend Dances, Movies and Places of ill reputation, all of which are destructive to their churches.

Presbytery
 The Presbytery shall issue Cards of Standing to its members upon presentation of a report in person or in case of sickness or some unavoidable hindrance letters may be accepted. A donation of $1.00 is required.

107th session 1950 - *Reverend Bayless McDonald dismissed in prayer.*

Presbytery
 Brothers J.C. Lynn and Ronald Creech were examined and we recommend them for ordination.

109th session 1952 - Wednesday afternoon – *N.R. Smith* read a portion of Hebrews 12:1. *Reverend Roger Reeds* dismissed in prayer.

110th session 1953 - *Reverend Lonnie Davoult made the benediction.*

Presbytery
Recommend that Billy Walker be ordained to the full gospel ministry.

111th session 1954 - *Reverend Bob King was welcomed into the association.*

112th session 1955 – The Presbytery ratified Robert E. Picirilli and Gordon Sebastian's credentials.

114th session 1957 – *Reverend and Mrs. Roy Thomas sang I'm Homesick for Heaven.*
 Willie Justice dismissed the Thursday morning session in prayer.

J.B. Fletcher and Jack Paramore were elected to the Foreign Missions Board.

115th session 1958 - Reverend Harold Harrison mentioned as being elected to the Association Foreign Missions Board.

117th session 1960 - Reverends Bob Ketchum, Tom Johnson, Harold Pitts and Bill Robinson mentioned for having parts in the Thursday morning session.

118th session 1961 - *Reverend J.D. O'Donnell delivered the message from John 12:23-32.*

Resolution – *Whereas the Cumberland Association owns 20 shares of stock in the Free Will Baptist Press of Ayden, NC, and whereas this Press is longer cooperating with our National Program: Be it resolved that this association instruct its officers to endeavor to get the money from this stock and donate it to the National Sunday School Board to assist them in launching their new literature program.*

119th session 1962 - *The moderator then presented Reverend J.L. Welch as the morning speaker. The body stood in tribute to Brother Welch, one of the denomination's leaders and one of the district pastors retiring from his years of serve at Cofer's Chapel church. Brother Welch used John 7:38 Come unto Me and drink and out of him shall flow rivers of living waters.*

Reverend Paul Ketteman, representative from the Bible College thanked the Association for its increased support and reported the work of the school. Reverend Archie Mayhew brought the Wednesday afternoon devotion.

120th session 1963 - *Reverend Harold Harrison, representing the Sunday School Department of the National Association, spoke on behalf of his work. Reverend Fred Hall led in singing. The Bible College Choir, led by Donald Clark, presented a short program. Reverend Richard Cordell presented the Nominating Committee report.*

122nd session 1965 - Reverend Ralph Hampton mentioned as serving on Hillmont Assembly Board of Directors.
Reverend Eugene Waddell led the Wednesday morning singing. Teddy Wilbanks was elected to a two-year term on the Hillmont Board of Directors. On Thursday afternoon, Reverend Don Sexton gave a report on the work at Chattanooga.

124th session 1967 - Reverend Earl Sutton led the music in the Thursday afternoon session.
Hillmont Camp – The Board be given authority to try to arrange a sale for our Hillmont grounds, expecting at least enough to cover present indebtedness, final details of the contract to be approved by the Executive Committee. Motion made, seconded and approved.

125th session 1968 - *Reverend George Lee led the congregational singing in the Wednesday morning sessions. The Earl Langley Family sang a special number Sweeter Each Day in the Thursday morning service.*

Hillmont Camp - We are happy to report the sale of the Hillmont property on December 16, 1967, to the National C.T.S. for $7,500. The $7,500 has been received, the bondholders have been paid off, and the title transferred.

Tennessee State Association - *The Association voted in the 1967 session to begin the publication of a state paper. This has been carried out and THE ECHO has been circulated to the churches throughout the year.*

126th session 1969 - Reverend Milton Crowson mentioned as serving on Education and Literature Board. Reverend John Gibbs serving on Home Missions Board and Herbert Peppers serving on the Superannuation Board.

127th session 1970 – *Reford Wilson was introduced as the Director of Foreign Missions. Bill Van Winkle was introduced as beginning a new work in Murfreesboro, TN. Eddie Vincent dismissed the morning session in prayer.*

131st session 1974 - *Reverend William Henry Oliver addressed the association to announce the celebration of his 50th anniversary of being an ordained FWB minister. He mentioned that 50 years ago at this Association time he was ordained. The minister-educator reported. The Associational Body rose in salute to Brother Oliver and passed a motion that this recognition should be recorded in the minutes.*

Notable Ordination Services in 1974
Glenn Poston – May 29, 1974 at Pardue Memorial Church
Tim McDonald – October 5, 1974 at Oak Grove Church
Jonathan Thigpen – at Cofer's Chapel Church

133rd session 1976 – Rock Music
The Temperance Committee has reported for well over 100 years. They presented a strong 2½ page single spaced statement on the problems with Rock Music. They named specific individuals, groups, songs and albums that should be avoided. The album "Goat's Head Soup," and groups: Grand Funk, Deep Purple, Led Zeppelin, The Rolling Stones. Individuals: Alice Cooper, Janice Joplin, David Bowie and Jimmy Hendrix to name a few. Interesting Report.

135th session 1978 - *Notable Ordinations* for the year: Garnett Reid, Roy Harris, Virgil Nolen, Alvin Hook, and Michael Carlisle.

136th session 1979 – *Five retired ministers were honored for a combined 243 years of service in their efforts for the Lord and the ministry: Earnest Craft, Luther Reed, J.B. Parson, John L. Welch and Henry Oliver. The congregation responded to this announcement with a standing ovation of appreciation.*
Notable Ordinations in 1979: Greg Bevan, *Jim Capshaw, Michael Carlisle, Duane Harvey, Rodney Outlaw, Richard Smith, Doug Thorp, Ricky Vaughn, Vernon Whaley, and Roy Woods.*

138th session 1981 – *Steve Hasty gave the report from Pleasant View Christian School. Joe Haas gave a report from Woodbine Christian Academy.*

145th session 1988 – *Bill Gardner, pastor of the Fellowship Church sang, "I'm Going Higher" and also "I'm Going Home."*
Brother David Simpson informed the Association that

54 years ago today, 10/11/1934 – 10/11/1988, Reverend Robert Crawford was ordained into the Gospel Ministry.

149th session 1992 - *The Moderator gave the Executive Committee instructions to make special plans for next year's 150th Annual Session.*

151st session 1994 – The Annual Meeting was moved from Tuesday to Saturday. *Be it resolved that beginning October of 1995 the Association meet on the second Saturday of October, and that the quarterly associations be asked to adjust their meeting times accordingly.*

156th session 1999 – *Jon Justice* begins his tenure as Moderator. *Motion MSC to move Cumberland Meeting from 2nd Saturday to 3rd Saturday beginning October 21, 2000.*

157th session 2000 – *Jerry Whitworth, Director of Cumberland Camp, gave the Camp Report.*

158th session 2001 – This was the first Cumberland Association meeting after the 9/11/2001 terrorist attack on America. *The tragedy was heavy on the Association members' minds.*

159th session 2002 - *A motion was MSC to oppose The Tennessee Lottery.*

160th session 2003 – *Gerald McAlister, new President of Tennessee State Master's Men, gave a report of what is taking place among laymen of the state.*

162nd Annual session – minutes not available

164th Annual session – 2007 minutes missing

165th session 2008 – Roy Harris elected Moderator for 2008-09.

166th session 2009 –
- *Constitution changed to extend officer terms to two years.*
- *Approved to develop a Cumberland Association website.*
- *Approved to place the minutes in PDF format on the website and do away with the printing of the minutes. The Clerk will place a hard copy in the Historical Archives at Free Will Baptist Bible College and also a digital copy will be kept.*

There were 62 churches in the Cumberland.

170th session 2013 – The Cumberland Association meeting was shortened and would be completed during the morning, doing away with the afternoon session.
The Presbytery began meeting during lunch instead of after the final session later in the day.

171st session 2014 – This was the first year of appointing committees before the day of the Cumberland meeting.

172nd session 2015 – The Nominating Committee met prior to the day of the meeting and selected individuals willing to serve on the various committees and also suggested board member nominations.

174th session 2017 –Ministerial Benevolence Board was revamped. A voluntary program to help Cumberland pastors and their wives, in case of death, was developed.

Names of the Cumberland Association

By

Roy W. Harris

The name of the Association changed a number of times throughout its 175-year history.

The Association was called Cumberland Association of Free-will Baptist Church of Christ at the 43rd session, October 16-19, 1886. The Association changed the name to Free-will Christian Baptist Church of Christ. The minutes recorded this motion which was seconded and passed by the body: *in order not to sacrifice title, name, neither any Church property, we assume to adopt the name Free-will Christian Baptist Church of Christ, thereby show the world that we are one people, and are consolidated in name. This done on the 18th day of October, A.D. 1886.*

The Association minutes from the 68th session in 1911 reveal a concern about mistakes having been made in receiving ministers from other denominations into the Association. The name of the Association written in the minutes was Freewill Christian Baptist of the Cumberland Association. The paragraph preceding the actual resolutions is as follows:

Resolved: Whereas we as Freewill Christian Baptist of the Cumberland Association have made mistakes in taking into our Presbytery as ministers, (from other denominations) who have done us much harm, and we therefore offer the following resolutions…

The name was eventually changed to the Cumberland Association of Freewill Baptists. The Freewill was separated into two words, Free and Will in the 89th session minutes in 1932.

The Association has been called The Cumberland Association of Free Will Baptists in the minutes since then.

Moderators, Clerks and General Information

By

Roy W. Harris

The first meeting of the Cumberland Association of Free Will Baptists took place in October 1843. The meeting was held at *Heads Meeting House* on Saturday through Monday. Elder William Barton delivered a sermon from Acts 10:34-35. Moderator William Barton, Clerk Wilson L. Gower were selected at the meeting. The offering totaled $7.32.

1844 – 1875

The minutes for sessions 2 – 32 were lost.

33rd Annual Session, October 14-17, 1876
Meeting was held at Heads FWB Church
Reverend S.H. Lancaster delivered the sermon.
Offering $21.05
Moderator Reverend S.H. Lancaster, Clerk D. Nichols Clerk.

34th Annual Session, October 19, 1877
Meeting held at Bethel Church, Dickson County, TN
G.W. Carney delivered the sermon from Romans 1:25.
Offering $15
Moderator Reverend G.R. Head, Secretary D. Nichols

35th Annual Session missing - 1878

36th Annual Session, October 19-20, 1879
Meeting was held at Bethlehem Church, Cheatham County, TN

T.C. Cofer delivered the sermon from John 13:34-35.
Offering $17.45
Moderator Reverend T.C. Cofer, Secretary Clerk D. Nichols

37th Annual Session – October 16 - 18, 1880
(*Cumberland Association of Free Will Baptists Church of Christ*)
Meeting was held at Rock Springs Church, Dickson County, TN.
J.W. Gower delivered the sermon from Ephesians 2:11-17.
Offering $18.35
Moderator G.W. Carney, Secretary D. Nichols

38, 39 and 40 Sessions missing.

41st Annual Session, October 18-20, 1884
(*Cumberland Association of Free Will Baptists Church of Christ*)
Meeting was held at Rock Springs Church, Dickson County, TN
Reverend H.C. Pace delivered the sermon from John 3:1.
Moderator G.R. Head, Assistant Moderator J.W. Gower, Clerk S.W. Patterson

42nd Annual Session – October 17-19, 1885
Meeting was held at Liberty Church, Stewart County, TN
Reverend H.C. Pace delivered the sermon from John 12:32.
Moderator REVEREND J.W. Gower, Clerk Bro. J.E. Hudgens

43rd Annual Session – October 16-19, 1886
(*Cumberland Association of Free Will Baptists Church of Christ*)
Meeting was held at Bethlehem Church, Cheatham County, TN.
Offering $23.75
Reverend W.T. Mosely delivered the sermon.
Moderator G.R. Head, Clerk J.E. Hudgens

47th Annual Session – October 16-19, 1890
Meeting held at Oakland Church, Davidson, County, TN.
Offering - No amount listed.
Reverend H.C. Pace delivered the sermon.
Moderator A.D. Williams, Clerk J.E. Hudgens

48, 49 and 50 Sessions Missing

51st Annual Session - October 25-27, 1894
(*Cumberland Association of Freewill Baptists*)
Meeting held at Orlinda Church, Robertson County, TN.
Offering $21.97
Reverend W.B. Stewart delivered the sermon from Amos 4:12.
Moderator Reverend G.R. Head, Clerk J.E. Hudgens

52nd Annual Session – October 24-26, 1895
Held at Rock Springs Church, Dickson County, TN.
Offering $27.03
Moderator G.W. Binkley, Clerk J.E. Hudgens
Reverend L. Hosale delivered the sermon from Luke 12:40.

53rd Annual Session – October 22-24, 1896
Meeting held at Cofer's Chapel, Nashville, TN.
Offering – No amount listed.
Moderator Elder J.L. Welch, Clerk J.E. Hudgens
Reverend J.E. Hudgens delivered the sermon from Romans 13:12.

54th Annual Session – October 21-23, 1897
Meeting held at Hickory Grove Church, Dickson County, TN
Moderator Reverend G.V. Frey, Clerk J.E. Hudgens
Reverend G.V. Frey delivered the sermon from Acts 16:30.

55th Annual Session, October 20-22, 1898
Meeting held at Hopewell Church, Montgomery County, TN
Offering $27.60
Moderator G.W. Carney, Clerk J.W. Carter
Reverend W. ROGERS delivered the sermon from James 1:27.

56th Annual Session – October 19-21, 1899
Meeting held at Heads Church, Robertson County, TN.
Offering $29.39
Moderator Reverend J.E. Hudgens, Clerk G.W. Bindley.
Reverend G.W. Carney delivered the sermon from 1 John 3:2.

57th Annual Session – October 25-27, 1900
Meeting held at Mt. Zion Church, Cheatham County, TN
Offering $36.55
Moderator G.V. Frey, Clerk E.F. Miles
G.V. Frey delivered the sermon from 2 Timothy 2:2-3.

58th Annual Session Minutes Missing – 1901

59th Annual Session – October 22-24, 1902
Meeting held at Bethel Church, Cheatham County, TN.
Offering $31.68
Moderator E.F. Miles, Clerk J.E. Hudgens
Reverend M.S. Crowe delivered the message from Genesis 4:10.

60th Annual Session – October 21-23, 1903
Meeting held at Antioch Church, Dickson County, TN
Offering $32.75
Moderator J.E. Hudgens, Clerk G.W. Fambrough
No Speaker mentioned for the sermon of the day.

61st Annual Session – October 19-21, 1904
Meeting held at Bethlehem Church, Cheatham County, TN.
Offering $11.60

Moderator J.E. Hudgens, Clerk E.F. Miles
M.S. Crowe delivered the sermon from Daniel 1:8.

62nd Annual Session – October 18-19, 1905
(Shift from 3 days down to 2 days)

Meeting held at Good Springs Church, Cheatham County, TN.
Offering $28.15
Moderator J.H. Hudgens, Clerk G.W. Fambrough
E.F. Miles preached the sermon from 1 Corinthians 13:13.

63rd Annual Session – October 24-25, 1906

Meeting held at Indian Mound Church, Stewart County, TN
Offering $27.53
Moderator J.E. Hudgens, Clerk G.W. Fambrough
J.E. Hudgins delivered the sermon from Romans 8:28.

64th Annual Session - October 23-25, 1907
(back to 3 days)

Meeting held at Stony Point Church, Dickson County, TN
Offering $33.35
Moderator D.T. Armstrong, Clerk G.E. Steppe
J.E. Hudgens delivered the sermon from Psalms 133:1.

65th Annual Session – October 14-16, 1908
Cumberland Association of Freewill Christian Baptist

Meeting held at Rock Springs Church, Sobel, Dickson County, TN
Offering – No amount listed.
Moderator W.W. Davis, Clerk G.E. Steppe
C.H. Pickle delivered the sermon from Titus 2:11.

66th Annual Session – October 13-15, 1909

Meeting at Oak Lawn Church, Cheatham County, TN
Offering $18.45
Moderator J.E. Hudgens, Clerk G.E. Steppe
G.E. Steppe delivered the sermon from John 3:14-15.

67th Annual Session – November 2-4, 1910
Meeting held at Pleasant Hill Church, Stewart County, TN
Offering $19.20
Moderator D.T. Armstrong, Clerk J.H. Oliver
D.T. Armstrong delivered the message from Philippians 3:14.

68th Annual Session – September 27-29, 1911
Meeting held at Cofer's Chapel Church, Nashville, TN
Offering $39.26
Moderator J.E. Hudgens, Clerk Mrs. H.P. Smith was the first lady elected as an officer.
E.S. Pruitt delivered the sermon from Psalm 23. *His sermon was very interesting.*

69th Annual Session - October 2-4, 1912
Meeting held at Mt. Zion Church, Cheatham County, TN
Offering $20.63
Moderator J.L. Welch, Clerk, Mrs. H.P. Smith
We were royally entertained by J.L. Welch from Philippians 3:7-15.

70th Annual Session - October 1-3, 1913
Held at Shady Grove Church, Montgomery County, TN.
Offering $41.69
Moderator J.E. Hudgens, Clerk Mrs. H.P. Smith
D.T. Armstrong delivered the sermon from Joshua 1:6.

71st Annual Session –
September 30 - October 2, 1914
Meeting at Oak Grove Church, Dickson County, TN
Offering $24.38
Moderator D.T. Armstrong, Clerk J.H. Oliver
A.D. Duncan delivered the sermon from Luke 9:35.

72nd Annual Session – October 20-22, 1915
Held at Dunbar's Chapel Church, Steward County, TN.

Offering $120.90
Moderator A.D. Duncan, Clerk J.H. Oliver
J.L. Welch delivered the sermon on 1 Corinthians 12:31.

73rd Annual Session – October 18-20, 1916
Held at New Hope Church, Cheatham County, TN.
Offering $39.24
Moderator E.F. Miles, Clerk J.H. Oliver
A.D. Duncan delivered the sermon on Matthew 4:4.

74th Annual Session – October 24-26, 1917
Moderator D.T. Armstrong, Clerk J.H. Oliver
Offering – No amount listed.
J.H. Oliver delivered the sermon from Matthew 21:22.

75th Annual Session - October 23-25, 1918
Meeting held at Heads Church, Robertson County, TN
Offering $47.90
Moderator J.E. Hudgens, Clerk J.H. Oliver
J.L. Welch delivered the sermon from Psalm 78:41.
Subject: Limitations of God's Power.

76th Annual Session - October 22-14, 1919
Meeting held at Bethel Church, Cheatham County, TN.
Offering $43.70
Moderator J.E. Hudgens, Clerk J.H. Oliver
A.D. Duncan delivered the sermon from John 13:34-35.

77th Annual Session – September 29-30, 1920
Meeting held at Rock Springs Church, Dickson County, TN.
Offering – No amount listed.
Moderator A.D. Duncan, Clerk J.H. Oliver
J.L. Welch delivered the sermon from 1 John 1:3.

78th Annual Session - October 19-21, 1921
Meeting held at Bethlehem Church, Cheatham County, TN.
Offering $58.68

Moderator J.E. Hudgens, Clerk J.H. Oliver
D.T. Armstrong delivered the sermon from Matthew 11:28.

79th Annual Session - October 18-20, 1922
Moderator J.E. Hudgens, Clerk Mamie Moery
Offering $42.83
J.L. Welch delivered the sermon from Genesis 3:4.

80th Annual Session - October 24-26, 1923
Moderator J.E. Hudgens, Clerk W.M. Henry Oliver
Offering $33.30
W.B. Davenport delivered the sermon from 1 Samuel 17:29.

81st Annual Session - October 22-24, 1924
Meeting held at Oak Lawn Church, Cheatham County, TN.
Offering $38.61
W. Henry Oliver delivered the sermon from Acts 1:8: Christianity's Conquering March.

82nd Annual Session – October 21-23, 1925
Meeting at Mt. Zion Church, Cheatham County, TN
Offering – No amount listed.
Moderator J.E. Hudgens, Clerk G.W. Fambrough
J.H. Oliver delivered the sermon from John 4:31.

83rd Annual Session - October 20-22, 1926
Held at Dunbar's Chapel Church, Stewart County, TN.
Moderator J.E. Hudgens, Clerk G.W. Fambrough
W.J. Paul delivered the sermon from John 3:5.

84th Annual Session – October 19-21, 1927
Held at Oakwood Church
Moderator D.T. Armstrong, Clerk L.O. Burroughs
D.T. Armstrong delivered the sermon from Acts 10:38.

85th Annual Session – October 24-26, 1928
Held at Shady Grove Church
Moderator J.L. Welch, Clerk L.O. Burroughs
J.L. Welch delivered the sermon.

86th Annual Session - October 24-25, 1929
Held at Scott's Chapel Church
Moderator J.L. Welch, Clerk L.O. Burroughs
Offering given by churches $57.15
J.H. Oliver delivered the sermon from Matthew 23:23.

87th Annual Session - October 22-24, 1930
Meeting at Oak Grove Church
Moderator J.L. Welch, Clerk L.O. Burroughs
Offering from churches $68.50
J.H. Oliver delivered the sermon from Matthew 18:3.

88th Annual Session - October 14-16, 1931
Meeting held at New Hope Church
Offering from churches $56.75
J.E. Hudgens Moderator, L.O. Burroughs Clerk.
J.L. Welch delivered the sermon from Hebrews 13:8.

89th Annual Session – October 12-14, 1932
Meeting held at Heads Church
Offering – No amount listed.
J.E. Hudgens Moderator, L.O. Burroughs Clerk
J.E. Hudgens delivered the sermon.

90th Annual Session – October 11-13, 1933
Meeting held at Bethel Church
Offering from Churches $44.80
J.L. Welch Moderator, L.O. Burroughs Clerk
J.E. Hudgens delivered the sermon from Psalms 126 and 133.

91st Annual Session - October 17-19, 1934
Meeting held at Brandon's Chapel
Offering $50.44
J.L. Welch Moderator, L.O. Burroughs Clerk
J.L. Welch delivered the sermon (Moderator's message) from Acts 13.

93rd Annual Session – October 14-16, 1936
Meeting held at Oaklawn Church
Offering – No amount listed.
J.L. Welch Moderator, L.O. Burroughs Clerk
W.J. Paul delivered the sermon from Acts 2:16.

94th Annual Session – October 13-15, 1937
Meeting held at Rock Springs Church, Dickson County, TN
Offering $54.75
J.E. Hudgens Moderator, L.O. Burroughs Clerk
J.E. Hudgens delivered the sermon.

95th Annual Session – October 12-14, 1938
Meeting held at Oak Grove Church, Dickson County, TN
Offering from churches for printing minutes $45.36
J.E. Hudgens Moderator, L.O. Burroughs Clerk
J.E. Hudgens delivered the sermon (Moderator's message)

96th Annual Session – October 11-13, 1939
Meeting held at Mt. Zion Church, Cheatham County
Offering – No amount listed.
J.E. Hudgens Moderator, L.O. Burroughs Clerk
W.B. Davenport delivered the message from Mark 9 and Luke 8.

97th Annual Session - October 17-18, 1940
Meeting held at Good Springs Church
Offering $51.45

J.E. Hudgens Moderator, L.O. Burroughs Clerk
L.O. Burroughs delivered the sermon from Psalm 133.

98th Annual Session – October 15-17, 1941
Meeting held at Heads Church, Ashland City, TN
Offering $65.25
J.E. Hudgens Moderator, L.O. Burroughs Clerk
G.M. Pruett delivered the sermon on Love.

99th Annual Session – October 14-15, 1942
Meeting held at Dunbar's Chapel, Stewart County, TN
J.E. Hudgens Moderator, L.O. Burroughs Clerk
J.E. Hudgens delivered the sermon.

100th Annual Session – October 13-14, 1943
Meeting held at New Hope Church, Cheatham County, TN
Offering – No amount listed.
J.E. Hudgens Moderator, Mrs. Huey Gower Clerk

101st Annual Session - October 11-12, 1944
Meeting held at Shady Grove Church, Montgomery County, TN
Offering $63.30.
E.A. Craft Assistant Moderator, Mrs. Huey Gower Clerk
Earnest Craft brought the sermon from Galatians 4:4: *But when the fullness of time was come, God sent for His Son, made of a woman, made under the law.*

102nd Annual Session – October 17-18, 1945
Meeting held at East Nashville Church, Davidson County, TN
Offering $133.00
E.A. Craft Moderator, Mrs. Huey Gower Clerk
Thursday morning session – Reverend Homer Willis brought a devotion.

103rd Annual Session - October 16-17, 1946
Meeting held at Craigfield Church, Hickman County, TN

Offering $100.11
J.L. Welch Moderator, Mrs. Huey Gower Clerk
L.R. Ennis delivered the sermon from Acts 2:1-4; 14:16.

104th Annual Session - October 15-16, 1947
Meeting held at Ashland City Church, Ashland City, TN
Offering – No amount listed.
J.L. Welch Moderator, Mrs. Huey Gower Clerk
Reverend L.C. Johnson, President of the Free Will Baptist Bible College brought the message from Acts 1:1-3.

106th Annual Session – October 12-13, 1949
Meeting held at Scott's Chapel Church
Monies received from the churches during the year: $448.16
J.L. Welch Moderator, Mrs. Nadyne Scott Acting Clerk
Reverend Charles Thigpen delivered the morning message from Jude 1:3 – *Contend for the Faith That Was Once Delivered Unto the Saints.*

107th Annual Session – October 11-12, 1950
Meeting held at Heads Church, Cedar Hill, TN
Income given by churches for the year: $264.78
E.A. Craft Moderator, Mrs. Byron Ross Clerk
C.F. Bowen delivered the message from John 14:6 – *I am the way, the truth, and the life, no man cometh unto the Father but by me.*

108th Annual Session – October 17-18, 1951
Meeting held at Good Springs Church, Pleasant View, TN
Monies given by churches for the year: $315.17
E.A. Craft Moderator, Mrs. Byron Ross Acting Clerk
C.B. Thompson delivered the morning message.

109th Annual Session – October 15-16, 1952
Meeting held at Rock Springs Church, Neptune, TN
Income from churches for the year: $272.40
E.A. Craft Moderator, Bayless McDonald Clerk

Bayless McDonald delivered the morning message from Acts 1:1-2 – *The Unfinished Task of Jesus.*

      110th Annual Session - October 14-15, 1953
Meeting held at Shady Grove Church, Hickory Point, TN
Monies received from churches: $293.20
E.A. Craft Moderator, Bayless McDonald Clerk
H.W. Davis brought the morning message from Luke 5:4 – *Launch Out Into the Deep.*

      111th Annual Session - October 13-14, 1954
Meeting held at Pleasant View, TN
Monies received from churches: $1,641.31
E.A. Craft Moderator, Bayless McDonald Clerk, Treasurer Mrs. J.B. Redding
Message delivered by Reverend Harold Pitts from 2 Corinthians 8:1-24 - *Proving the Sincerity of Your Love.*

      112th Annual Session – October 12-13, 1955
Meeting held at Pleasant Ridge Church, McEwen, TN
Offering $312.61
E.A. Craft Moderator, Bayless McDonald Clerk, Mrs. J.B. Redding Treasurer
Randy Cox delivered the message from Philippians 3:10 – *That I May Know Him.*

      113th Annual Session – October 17-18, 1956
Meeting held at Good Springs Church, Pleasant View, TN
Offering $299.25
Luther Reed Moderator, E.B. McDonald Clerk, Mrs. J.B. Redding Treasurer
J.L. Welch delivered the message from Psalm 12 – *Help Lord.*
ATTENDANCE – Delegates 19, Ministers 25, Visitors 151, Deacons 10 - Total 205.

      114th Annual Session – October 16-17, 1957

Meeting held at Gorman Church, McEwen, TN
Offering: No amount listed.
Luther Reed Moderator, E.B. McDonald Clerk, Mrs. J.B. Redding Treasurer
Reverend and Mrs. Roy Thomas sang, *I'm Homesick for Heaven*
Charles A. Thigpen, Dean of Free Will Baptist Bible College delivered the morning message from John 1:42 - *The Recoverability of Sinners.*

115th Annual Session - October 15-16, 1958
Meeting held at Carlisle Church, Carlisle, TN
Offering $365.40
Luther Reed Moderator, E.B. McDonald Clerk, Mrs. J.B. Redding Treasurer
Reverend Guy Owens, host pastor, welcomed the association to the Carlisle Church.
Louis Moulton, Promotional Worker for the National Foreign Missions Board, brought the morning message.
ATTENDANCE - Churches reporting 40, Ministers registered 42, Deacons registered 11, Delegates registered 61 and Visitors registered 50. TOTAL present 164.

116th Annual Session - October 14-15, 1959
Meeting held at Donelson Church, Donelson, TN
Offering No amount listed.
Luther Reed Moderator, E.B. McDonald Clerk, Mrs. J.B. Redding Treasurer
J.L. Welch brought the message from John 13:34-35 - *Things That Identify Us As Followers Of Christ.*
ATTENDANCE - 269

117th Annual Session –October 12-13, 1960
Meeting held at Scott's Chapel Church, Erin, TN.
Offering $349
Luther Reed Moderator, E.B. McDonald Clerk

Reverend Charles A. Thigpen delivered the morning message from Luke 12:49-53; Ephesians 6:10-18: *Militant Christianity*. *A most rigorous message of challenge to ministers. An altar prayer was held with ministers rededicating their lives to preach God's truth as given in His Word.*
ATTENDANCE – 204

       118th Annual Session - October 17-18, 1961
Meeting held at Oaklawn Church, Pleasant View, TN
Offering $389.40
Luther Reed Moderator, E.B. McDonald Clerk
Reverend J.D. O'Donnell delivered the message from John 12:23-32.
ATTENDANCE - 333

       119th Annual Session – October 17-18, 1962
Meeting held at Stony Point Church, Van Leer, TN
Offering $395
W.B. Hughes Moderator, E.B. McDonald Clerk
The moderator then presented Reverend J.L. Welch as the morning speaker. The body stood in tribute to Brother Welch, one of the denomination's leaders and one of the district pastors retiring from his years of serving at Cofer's Chapel church. Brother Welch used John 7:38 Come unto Me and drink and out of Him shall flow rivers of living waters.
Reverend Archie Mayhew brought the Wednesday afternoon devotion.
ATTENDANCE – 281

       120th Annual Session – October 16-17, 1963
Meeting held at Bethlehem Church, Ashland City, TN
Offering $100 *Motion- MSP to give the offering to help with the Bible College's indebtedness.*
W.B. Hughes Moderator, E.B. McDonald Clerk

Dean Charles A. Thigpen delivered the morning message from Acts 5:1-7.
ATTENDANCE – 301

      121st Annual Session - October 14-15, 1964
Meeting held at Brandon's Chapel, Bumpus Mills, TN
Offering - No amount listed.
Henry Melvin Moderator, Mrs. Robert Picirilli Clerk
ATTENDANCE – 291

      122nd Annual Session – October 12-13, 1965.
Held at West Nashville Church, Nashville, TN.
Offering - No amount listed.
Henry Melvin Moderator, Mrs. Robert Picirilli Clerk
Paul Ketteman delivered the message from Proverbs 29:18 and Amos 8:11-13

      123rd Annual Session – October 12-13, 1966
Meeting held at Rock Springs Church, Charlotte, TN
Offering $633.37
Rolla Smith Moderator, Mrs. Robert Picirilli Clerk
Reverend Gordon Hart brought the Wednesday morning message from Luke 9:52-62.
Reverend Nedo Eaddy brought the Wednesday afternoon message.
ATTENDANCE – 239

      124th Annual Session – October 11-12, 1967
Meeting held at Oak Grove Church, Charlotte, TN
Offering - No amount listed.
Ronald Niebruegge Moderator, Mrs. Robert Picirilli Clerk
ATTENDANCE – 274

      125th Annual Session - October 16-17, 1968
Meeting held at Woodbine Church, Nashville, TN
Offering - No amount listed.
Nedo Eaddy Moderator, W.B. Hughes Clerk
ATTENDANCE – 216

126th Annual Session –October 1969
Meeting at Heads Church, Cedar Hill, TN
Offering - No amount listed.
Wallace Hayes Moderator, W.B. Hughes Clerk

127th Annual Session – October 1970
Meeting held at Dickson First, Dickson, TN
Offering - No amount listed.
Wallace Hayes Moderator, W.B. Hughes Clerk
Harvey Hill brought the morning message from Acts 2:37-47.

128th Annual Session – October 12-14, 1971
Meeting held at Grace Church, Nashville, TN
Offering $148.48
Wallace Hayes Moderator, W.B. Hughes Clerk
Fred Hersey brought the morning message from Song of Solomon 7:10-13.
Bob Tremble led the opening song.
Don Lamb brought the morning devotion from Psalm 1
ATTENDANCE – 218

129th Annual Session – October 11-12, 1972
Meeting held at Bethlehem Church, Ashland City, TN
R. Eugene Waddell Moderator, W.B. Hughes Clerk
Offering $148.48
Don Lamb brought the morning message.
Fred Hall led the music.

130th Annual Session – October 17-18, 1973
Meeting held at Rock Springs Church, Charlotte, TN
Offering $181.98
R. Eugene Waddell Moderator, W.B. Hughes Clerk
Reverend Milton Worthington brought the morning devotion.
Reverend Hughes Ellis delivered the morning message from Genesis 17:1.
Reverend Joe Bragg closed in prayer.

131st Annual Session - October 16-17, 1974
Meeting held at East Nashville Church, Nashville, TN
Offering $198.50
John Gibbs Moderator, Reverend Albert Halbrook Clerk
ATTENDANCE – Registered 198, Churches 51
Reverend Bob Shockey gave the National Home Missions report.
Morning session recessed to the worship service by Reverend Jim Turnbough.
Reverend Joe Ange delivered the morning message from Mark 5:25 and Isaiah 6.
Reverend Tim McDonald brought the Thursday morning devotion.

132nd Annual Session - October 15-16, 1975
Meeting held at Good Springs Church, Pleasant View, TN
Offering $284.31
David Hicks Moderator, E.B. McDonald Clerk
Reverend Gary Lovit led in prayer.
The host pastor Reverend J.D. Norris welcomed everyone.
Reverend Ken Haney and Reverend Roy Helms led in prayers and Brother Steve Ashby from the FWBBC Music Department sang the special.
ATTENDANCE – 267

133rd Annual Session – October 12-14, 1976
Meeting held at Stoney Point Church, Vanleer, TN
Offering $188.47
David Hicks Moderator, Bill Van Winkle Clerk
Reverend Nate Ange delivered the morning message from Isaiah 6:2-12.
Brother Delbert Wood "Woody" gave the Cumberland Association Home Mission Board report.
Reverend Marion Pettus led singing and filled a number of roles at this meeting.
ATTENDANCE - 391

134th Annual Session – October 11-13, 1977
Meeting held at Richland Church, Nashville, TN
Offering $128.71
Marion Pettus Assistant Moderator, Bill Van Winkle Clerk
Reverend Ed Gragg Assistant Pastor welcomed the Association.
Reverend Ed Cook brought the Thursday morning message from Joshua 24:14-16.
Barney Hicks gave the Executive Board report.
Reverend Ron Parker gave the Petitions and Request report.
Reverend Tommy Street gave Temperance Committee report.
Reverend Herman Pannell gave Nominations Committee report.
ATTENDANCE – 317

135th Annual Session – October 1978
Meeting held at Oaklawn Church, Woodlawn, TN
Offering - No amount listed.
Wallace Hayes Moderator, Barney Hicks Clerk
Reverend Garnett Reid gave the Committee on Committees report.
Reverend Eugene Workman brought the Wednesday morning message.
Notable Ordinations for the year: Garnett Reid, Roy Harris, Virgil Nolen, Alvin Hook and Michael Carlisle.

136th Annual Session October 16-17, 1979
Meeting held at First Church McEwen, McEwen, TN
Offering $225.41
Eugene Waddell Moderator, Garnet Reid Clerk
Reverend Jim Walker, pastor of the Woodbine Church, gave the Wednesday evening message.
Reverend Roger Hood gave the report for Pleasant View Christian School.

Reverend Ronnie Smith gave the Obituary Committee report.
Reverend David Williford gave the Petitions and Requests Committee report.
ATTENDANCE – 324

        137th Annual Session – October 14-15, 1980
Meeting held at Faith Church, Columbia, TN
Offering $225.71
Vernon Barker Moderator, Joe Grimmett Clerk
Reverend Danny Dwyer led opening prayer.

        138th Annual Session – October 1981
Meeting held at Bethel Church, Ashland City, TN
Offering $210.83
Roy Helms Moderator, Ken Haney Clerk
Reverend Wendall Walley brought the Tuesday morning devotion.
Reverend Robert Morgan responded to the welcome from the host pastor on behalf of the Association.
ATTENDANCE - 353

        139th Annual Session – October 12-13, 1982
Meeting held at Gorman Church, Waverly, TN
Offering $223.09
ATTENDANCE – 307
Raymond Riggs Moderator, Ray Prince Clerk
Reverend Vernon Barker brought the Tuesday 9:00 a.m. morning message.
Layman Trymon Messer brought the Tuesday 11:00 a.m. message.
Reverend Terry Boyd gave the Committee on Committees report.
Reverend Paul Sitton brought the Tuesday evening message.
Dr. Robert Woodard brought the Wednesday 9:00 a.m. morning message.

140th Annual Session – October 11-12, 1983
Meeting held at Richland Church, Nashville, TN
Offering $137.60
ATTENDANCE - 258
Larry Clyatt Moderator, Ray Prince Clerk
Cumberland Youth Camp Board was given permission to hire a Camp Director.
Reverend Tim Trimble led the opening song.
Reverend Roy Roach extended greetings and welcome from the host church.
Reverend Sam McVay gave a partial report of the Cumberland Youth Camp Board.

141st Annual Session - October 16-17, 1984
Meeting held at Ashland City Church, Ashland City, TN
Offering $194.76
ATTENDANCE - 263
Larry Clyatt Moderator, Randall Riggs Clerk
Reverend Gene Outland, new pastor of Cofer's Chapel Church brought the 9:00 a.m. message from Ezekiel 3:1-18.
Reverend Tim Young, pastor of the Gorman Church led in prayer at the 11:00 a.m. service.

142nd Annual Session - October 15-16, 1985
Meeting held at United Church, Dickson, TN
Offering $265.55
ATTENDANCE – 245
Robert Crawford Moderator, Randall Riggs Clerk
Reverend Wayne Bess pastor of First Dickson Church brought the 9:00 a.m. message.
Reverend Jesse Meade, pastor of Loyal Chapel Church brought the Tuesday evening message.
Missionary appointee Donnie McDonald dismissed the 11:00 a.m. worship service in prayer.
Cumberland Youth Camp Board hired Reverend Marion Pettus as Camp Manager/Director.

143rd Annual Session – October 14-15, 1986
Meeting held at East Nashville Church, Nashville, TN
Offering $198.48
ATTENDANCE - 197
Robert Crawford Moderator, Randall Riggs Clerk
Morning message delivered by Maxie Milliken from Matthew 4:5.
Glenn Poston preached on Tuesday morning from Hebrews 11:1-27.

144th Annual Session – October 13-14, 1987
Meeting held at Good Springs Church, Pleasant View, TN
Offering $150.95
ATTENDANCE - 261
Robert Crawford Moderator, Randall Riggs Clerk
Morning message was delivered by Robert Morgan from Romans 8:26-19.
Wayne Wagnor was appointed as chairman of the Committee on Committees.

145th Annual Session – October 11-12, 1988
Meeting held at Rock Springs Church, Dickson, TN
    Cumberland Program changed from 2 days to 1 day.
MSC that the Cumberland Association Annual Meeting hereafter schedule its entire program in one day.
Offering $200
ATTENDANCE - 131
Robert Crawford Moderator, Clayton Hampton Clerk
Daryl Ellis, pastor of Cross Timbers Church, led in prayer before the Tuesday morning message.
Eddie Hodges, pastor of the Hendersonville Church, delivered the morning message from 1 Corinthians 1:1-17.
Chris Real, pastor of Horton Heights Church, led in prayer at the morning worship service.
Missionary to France Allen Crowson delivered the Tuesday morning message.
Ken Dodson, pastor of Woodbine FWB Church, brought the Wednesday morning message from 1 Corinthians 3:1-9.

146th Annual Session – October 10, 1989
Meeting held at Loyal Chapel Church, Columbia, TN
Offering $176
ATTENDANCE - 98
Robert Crawford Moderator, Clayton Hampton Clerk
Larry Powell gave the Tennessee State Home Mission Board report.
John Gibbs ministered in song.
Carlos Kelsey led in prayer to begin the afternoon session.
Pete Winstead, pastor of Trinity Church in Bowling Green, KY delivered the afternoon message from Colossians 1:18.

147th Annual Session – October 9, 1990
Meeting held at Ashland City Church, Ashland City, TN
Offering $110.50
ATTENDANCE - 112
Gerald Fender was recognized to bring information on the mission work he is establishing in Knoxville.
Donnie McDonald, Missionary to Japan, brought the morning message from 1 Peter 2:9-10.
Ron Helms gave the Nominating Committee report.
Jimmy Carrington gave the Resolutions Committee report.

148th Annual Session – October 8, 1991
Meeting held at Hurricane Chapel Church, McEwen, TN
Offering $104.84
ATTENDANCE - 133
Fred Hall Moderator, Clayton Hampton Clerk
Jimmy Carrington brought the morning message.
Dicky Anderson led in prayer after a song at the beginning of the afternoon session.
Ken Riggs delivered the afternoon message.

149th Annual Session – October 13, 1992
Meeting held at Sylvan Park Church, Nashville, TN
Offering $84.86
ATTENDANCE - 72

Fred Hall Moderator, Clayton Hampton Clerk
Chris Truett and Donald Myers from FWBBC brought the special music for the morning worship service.
Dr. Robert Picirilli brought the morning message from 2 Timothy 3:14-17, 2 Peter 1:20-21.
Barry Simpson brought the Petitions report.

150th Annual Session – October 12, 1993
Meeting held at Cumberland Camp, Woodlawn, TN
Offering $86
ATTENDANCE - 84
Fred Hall Moderator, Clayton Hampton Clerk
Homer Willis brought the morning message from Jeremiah 6:16, Luke 5:39.
Steve Faison brought a special in song before the afternoon message.
Terry Eagleton gave the Petitions and Requests Committee report.

151st Annual Session – October 11, 1994
Meeting held at First Dickson Church, Dickson, TN
Offering $100
ATTENDANCE - 84
Fred Hall Moderator, Steve Lindsey Clerk
Danny Thompson delivered the morning message in the 9:00 a.m. service from Genesis 39:1-12.
Mike Nabors brought the message in the 11:00 a.m. from Jeremiah 18:1-6,15.
David Baker gave the Petitions and Requests Committee report.

152nd Annual Session – October 14, 1995
Meeting held at Horton Heights Church, Nashville, TN
Offering $85.30
ATTENDANCE - 68
Fred Hall Moderator, Clayton Hampton Clerk
Jonathan Kell led the music and Randy Fosse accompanied at the piano.

Randy Corn brought the 9:00 a.m. message from
2 Timothy 3:15-17.
Leroy Forlines bought the 11:00 a.m. message sharing Ten Characteristics of God using several Scriptures.
Mike Gillock gave the Petitions and Requests Committee report.
Randy Skaggs gave the Registration and Finance Committee report.
Eric Bowen gave the Resolutions and Finance report.

153rd Annual Session – October 12, 1996
Meeting held at Cumberland Camp, Woodlawn, TN
Offering $161.00
ATTENDANCE - 106
Fred Hall Moderator, Clayton Hampton Clerk
Derek Bell brought greetings from the newly formed South Central Quarterly and then brought the 9:00 a.m. worship service message from 2 Corinthians 5:20.
Bob Bagget gave the Obituary Committee report.
Rick Futch gave the Petitions and Requests report.
Greg Tyson gave the Registration and Finance report.
Cecil Boswell gave the Nominating Committee report.

154th Annual Session – October 11, 1997
Meeting held at Dunbar's Chapel Church, Indian Mound, TN
Offering $93.06
ATTENDANCE - 78
Fred Hall Moderator, Greg Tyson Clerk
Steve Parks led the singing at the 11:00 a.m. service.
Ronald Mashburn, pastor of Crossroads Church in the South Central Quarterly, brought the 11:00 a.m. worship service message.
Larry Montgomery, pastor of Cofer's Chapel Church, brought the afternoon devotion from Revelation 1:12:17.

155th Annual Session – October 10, 1998
Meeting held at Trinity Church, Nashville, TN
Offering $109

ATTENDANCE - 82
Fred Hall Moderator, Greg Tyson Clerk
Joe Hurst and Harold Harrison gave the Obituary Committee report.

156th Annual Session – October 9, 1999
Meeting at Loyal Chapel Church, Columbia, TN
Offering $156.75
ATTENDANCE - 89
Jon Justice Moderator, Eddie Hodges Clerk
Chris Moody, pastor of Oak Grove Church brought the 9:00 a.m. devotion.
Duane James led the music for the 11:00 a.m. service.
Dr. James Cox, Director of Institutional Effectiveness at FWBBC, brought the 11:00 a.m. message from Hebrews 9:24.
Randy Kinnick gave the Obituary Committee report.
Rodney Staford gave the Resolutions Committee report.

157th Annual Session – October 21, 2000
Meeting held at Ashland City Church, Ashland City, TN
Offering $161
ATTENDANCE - 69
Jon Justice Moderator, Eddie Hodges Clerk
Len Scott opened the singing for the 9:00 a.m. session.
Steve Swango delivered the 9:00 a.m. message from James 5:13-18.
Jerry Whitworth, Director of Cumberland Camp, gave the Camp report.
Gary Lovitt delivered the 11:00 a.m. message from Galatians 5:7-13.
Stan Coker delivered the 1:00 p.m. message from Romans 15:7.
Kent Barwick brought the Petitions and Requests report.

158th Annual Session – October 20, 2001
Meeting held at United Church, Dickson, TN
Offering - No amount listed

ATTENDANCE - Not listed.
Jon Justice Moderator, Eddie Hodges Clerk
This was the first Association meeting since the 9/11/2001 terrorist attack on America. The tragedy was heavy on Association members' minds.
Tom McCullough brought the 1:00 p.m. message from Luke 14:22.

159th Annual Session - October 15, 2002
Meeting held at Cofer's Chapel Church, Nashville, TN
Offering $125
ATTENDANCE - 80
Jon Justice Moderator, Eddie Hodges Clerk
Matthew Pinson, new President of Free Will Baptist Bible College, gave a report on the college.
Frank Owens gave a report on the College Alumni Project.
A motion was MSC to oppose the Tennessee Lottery.

160th Annual Session – October 14, 2003
Meeting held at Berean Church, Fairview, TN
Offering $119
ATTENDANCE - 67
Jon Justice Moderator, Eddie Hodges Clerk
Matt McAffee, pastor of New Life Church in Columbia, TN, brought the 9:00 a.m. message from 1 Thessalonians 1:5-10.
David Outlaw, pastor of Heads Church, brought the 11:00 a.m. message from 1 Thessalonians 2:1-12.
Gerald McAlister, new President of Tennessee State Master's Men, gave a report of what is taking place among laymen of the state.
Cliff Donoho gave an invitation to the Presbytery Ministers' Retreat in March.

161st Annual Session –October 16, 2004
Meeting held at Bethel Church, Ashland City, TN
Offering $184
ATTENDANCE - 81

Jon Justice Moderator, Eddie Hodges Clerk
James Black, pastor of Miller's Chapel Church, brought the 11:00 a.m. message from Mark 16:15.
Doug Dicky, pastor of Flatwoods Church brought the 1:00 p.m. message from Acts 20:7-11.

163rd Annual Session –October 21, 2006
Meeting held at Woodbine Church, Nashville, TN
Offering $182.54
ATTENDANCE - 81
Churches in the Cumberland: Northern Quarterly – 23, South Central – 7, Southern – 16, Western – 15, Total Churches 61
Jon Justice Moderator, Patrick Layton, Clerk
Ed Fox delivered the morning message.

165th Annual Session – October 18, 2008
Meeting held at Ashland City Church, Ashland City, TN
Offering $330
ATTENDANCE - 118
Jon Justice Moderator, Patrick Layton, Clerk
Roy Harris elected Moderator for 2008-09
Donnie McDonald, Missionary to Japan, delivered the morning devotion.
Bobby Pool, Missionary to Brazil, delivered the morning message.

166th Annual Session – October 17, 2009
Meeting held at Ashland City Church, Ashland City, TN
Offering $203
ATTENDANCE - 102
Roy Harris Moderator, Patrick Layton Clerk
There were 62 Churches in the Cumberland.
Barry Simpson from International Missions delivered morning message.
Bert Tippett delivered the afternoon message.
The Constitution was changed to extend officer terms to two years.

- Approved to develop a Cumberland Association website.
- Approved to place the minutes in PDF format on the website and do away with the printing of the minutes. The Clerk will place a hard copy in the Historical Archives at Free Will Baptist Bible College and also keep a digital copy.

167th Annual Session – October 16, 2010
Meeting held at Rejoice Church, Antioch, TN
Offering $344
ATTENDANCE - 84
There were 60 churches in the Cumberland.
Roy Harris Moderator, Patrick Layton Clerk
Randy Riggs delivered the morning message.
Frank Owens delivered the afternoon message.

168th Annual Session – October 15, 2011
Meeting held at Ashland City Church, Ashland City, TN
Offering $241
ATTENDANCE - 96
Churches in the Cumberland: 62
Roy Harris moderator, Patrick Layton Clerk
Tim Farris delivered the morning message.
Randy Corn delivered the afternoon message.

169th Annual Session – October 20, 2012
Meeting held at Pleasant View Christian School, Pleasant View, TN
Offering: $140
ATTENDANCE: 86
There were 59 churches in the Cumberland.
Roy Harris Moderator, Patrick Layton Clerk
David Womack delivered the morning message.
Chad Kivette delivered the afternoon message.

170th Annual Session – October 19, 2013
Meeting held at Hurricane Chapel Church

Offering $325
ATTENDANCE - 71
There were 59 churches in the Cumberland.
Dr. Roy Harris Moderator, Patrick Layton Clerk
Jason Willaford delivered the morning message.
- Shortened the session to be completed during the morning. Did away with the afternoon session.
- Moved the Presbytery Meeting from after the Cumberland Session to meet during lunch.

171st Annual Session – October 18, 2014
Meeting held at Cane Ridge Church, Antioch, TN
Offering $1,200 - Offering will be given to Wallace and Judy Hayes.
ATTENDANCE - 82
Dr. Roy Harris Moderator, Patrick Layton Clerk
Dr. Roy W. Harris delivered the morning message.
First year Association Committees were appointed in advance of the Cumberland Meeting day.

172nd Annual Session – October 17, 2015
Meeting held at the Cumberland Camp, Woodlawn, TN
Offering $644
ATTENDANCE - 76
There were 60 churches in the Cumberland.
Dr. Roy Harris Moderator, Patrick Layton Clerk
Dr. Robert Morgan delivered the morning message.
Nominating Committee met prior to the day of the meeting and selected individuals to serve on the various committees and also suggested board member nominations.

173rd Annual Session – October 15, 2016
Meeting held at 180 FWB Church, Clarksville, TN
Offering $498
ATTENDANCE - 80
There were 60 churches in the Cumberland.
Dr. Roy Harris Moderator, Patrick Layton Clerk
Dr. Danny Dwyer delivered the morning message.

174th Annual Session – October 21, 2017
Meeting held at First Church Dickson, Dickson, TN
Offering $280
ATTENDANCE - 92
There were 60 churches in the Cumberland.
Dr. Roy Harris Moderator, Patrick Layton Clerk
Dr. Matthew J. Pinson, Welch College President, delivered the morning message.

Quarterly Meetings of the Cumberland Association

By
Roy W. Harris

The Cumberland Association began efforts to form local, smaller groups of churches within its ranks as early as 1898. Minutes from the 55th session in 1898 record the following motion:

The churches in the country be grouped together, consisting of 2, 3 or not more than 4. Each group shall compose a circuit. If in town and the church strong enough to support a preacher to be called a station.

That in the midst of the groups, as near the center as possible, a parsonage be built for the preacher, each church contributing its part of the labor or money. This shall be done as soon as the brethren composing the group think they are able to do it.

That the ministers and deacons of the Cumberland Association shall consult together at each ministers' and deacons' meeting for the purpose of grouping the churches until satisfactory arrangements can be made and final report and work completed by the next Association.

A much stronger effort was made in 1924. The following is recorded in the 81st session minutes from the Committee on Fifth Sunday Union Meetings:
We recommend that our churches be divided into districts as follows:

- *Western Division – Brandon's Chapel, Dunbar's Chapel, Emanuel's Chapel, Hurricane Chapel, Indian Mound, Midway, Pleasant Hill, Scott's Chapel, Smith's Grove, Stony Point and Union Hill.*

- *Middle Division – Bethel, Bethlehem, Good Springs, Heads, Maple Valley, Miller's Chapel, Oak Grove, Oak Lawn, Oakwood, Olivet, Rock Springs and Shady Grove.*

- *Eastern Division – Cofer's Chapel, Craigfield, Greenwood, Marrowbone, Mt. Pleasant, Mt. Zion, New Hope, Oakland, Royal's Chapel, Spring Hill and West Nashville.*

It appears ten years later in 1934 that more needed to be done to better organize the quarterly meetings. Reverend Henry Oliver was elected Supervisor of the Quarterly Meetings during the 91st session. The minutes recorded the following:

On motion, the matter of grouping the various churches, each church appoint their own delegate to the quarterly meeting and state (announce) whom they want to be grouped with.

Brother Oliver did a great job in moving the process forward. The 1935 minutes list three districts (Quarterlies) with a total of 33 churches: Eastern District – 10 churches; Central District - 17 churches; Western Division 6 churches.

The Association took another major step forward three years later in 1938 with the appointment by the Cumberland Moderator of Chairmen for the three Divisions (Quarterlies). Reverend E.A. Craft was appointed Chairman of the Eastern Division. Reverend W.B. Davenport was appointed Chairman of the Central Division.

Reverend G.M. Pruett was appointed Chairman of the Western Division.

The report at the 96th session in 1939 revealed slow progress. The Eastern Division, what is now basically the Southern Quarterly, met three times. Note: Not so much interest in them. The Western Division reported two meetings. Note: Large crowds with lots of interest shown.

The 1955 minutes of the 112th session listed 29 churches in the *Eastern Division* and 15 churches in the *Western Division.* These two Divisions became the dominant ones and little is recorded about the *Central Division.*

The *Divisions* of the Association are called *Quarterlies* for the first time in the 1957, 114th session minutes.

A glimpse of the importance of the *Quarterlies* can be seen in those same minutes. A constitutional change designated the Quarterly Meetings as the avenue for membership in the Cumberland Association. Churches before 1957 petitioned the Association directly for membership. The minutes recorded the following:

Motion made and passed to amend the constitution: *New churches shall petition the quarterly meeting for membership."*

1967 was a pivotal year in the development of quarterly meetings within the Cumberland Association. The 124th session minutes recorded the following:

The Eastern Quarterly Meeting met on January 14, 1967 to dissolve and form two new quarterlies: The Northern Quarterly and The Southern Quarterly.

The Southern Quarterly Meeting was organized on Saturday, January 14, 1967 at the Good Springs FWB Church, Pleasant View, TN.

Reverend Wallace Hayes gave the report of the Western Quarterly Meeting.

Reverend Eugene Waddell gave the report of the Southern Quarterly Meeting.

Reverend Kenneth Stephens gave the report of the Northern Quarterly Meeting.

Wallace Hayes, Western Quarterly; Glen Hood, Northern Quarterly; and Jerry Pinkerton, Southern Quarterly gave reports the next year in 1968 during the 125th session of the Cumberland Association.

1978 brought another major change for the Cumberland Association. The Association approved a change to the Cumberland Association Constitution that delegated more responsibility to the Quarterly Meetings. The Association authorized each Quarterly Meeting to set up their own *Examining Committees.*

This was a major change. Candidates for licensure and ordination would now be handled within the Quarterlies instead of coming directly to the Cumberland. The *Quarterly Examining Committees* would report their activities to the *Cumberland Association Presbytery*.

Recorded in the 135th session minutes in 1978:

Amendment made to the Cumberland Constitution to allow each Quarterly to set up its own Examining Committee. The amendment passed by a 2/3 vote.

A major step was taken in 1986 as recorded in the 143rd session minutes. The constitution was amended to; *require at least one board member must come from each quarterly of the Cumberland Association.*

The next major event that impacted the Quarterly Meetings occurred in 1995 during the 152nd session. The Cumberland Association voted to allow the Southern Quarterly to divide into two Quarterlies.

This division occurred between the 152nd and 153rd sessions. One Quarterly maintained the original name; *The Southern Quarterly* and the new quarterly adopted the name; *The South Central Quarterly*.

Derek Bell brought greetings from the newly formed *South Central Quarterly* to the 153rd session of the Cumberland in 1996. He also brought the 9:00 worship service message from 2 Corinthians 5:20.

The *South Central Quarterly* formally petitioned for membership in the Cumberland Association during the business session. Motion made, seconded and carried to accept the *South Central Quarterly* into the Cumberland Association.

163rd session minutes in 2006 listed the following: *Northern Quarterly 23, South Central Quarterly 7, Southern Quarterly 16, Western Quarterly 15 for at total of 61* churches in the Cumberland *Association.*

Churches and Pastors

By

Roy W. Harris

The minutes of the Cumberland Association of Free Will Baptists record the actions of the Association in receiving, petitionary letters, corresponding letters and motions to receive churches into the Association.

A chronological listing of actions by the Association of receiving churches into the Association is written below.

The numbers of churches and pastors at various times in the history of the Cumberland Association are also listed.

The information below is written exactly the way it appears in the minutes. This includes but is not limited to; churches, pastors, meeting sessions and years.

57th session 1900 - Indian Mound Church, Stewart County, TN, was received into the Association.

62nd session 1905 - *Petitionary Letters & Corresponding Letters*: Petitionary letter received and read from Oakwood Church, Robertson County then given to Committee on Petitions and Requests. Cumberland Association voted to receive the Oakwood Church, Thursday morning, October 19th 1905.

Cumberland Association Churches in 1905
Antioch, Bethel, Bethlehem, Brandon's Chapel, Charity, Cofer's Chapel, Cross Roads, Good Springs, Greenwood, Harpeth Valley, Heads, Hickory Grove, Hopewell, Hurricane

Chapel, Maple Valley, Mt. Liberty, Mt. Pleasant, Mt. Zion, Indian Mound, New Hope, Oak Grove, Oakland, Oak Lawn, Oakwood, Olivet, Pleasant Hill, Paradise Ridge, Pleasant Grove, Pleasant Valley, Rock Springs, Smith's Grove, Stony Point and Walnut Grove.

63rd session 1906 - Petitionary Letters and Corresponding Letters:
Petitionary Letters received from Miller's Chapel Church, Dickson County, TN and Spring Hill Church, Robertson County, TN requesting to become part of the Cumberland Association. Both were welcomed into the Association on Thursday afternoon.

Pleasant Grove Church petitioned to change its name in the Association from Pleasant Grove to Shady Grove. The petition was granted.

64th session 1907 - Petitions: Petition received from Scott's Chapel, Stewart County, TN to become part of the Cumberland Association. Voted to be received into the Association. 25 Churches represented at the meeting.

70th session 1913 – Petitions: That the petitions of Pruitt's Chapel Church and Union Hill Church be admitted into the Cumberland Association and their delegates be seated.

72nd session 1915 - Petition: We recommend Shaw's Chapel Church be received into the Association. Miller's Grove Church (formally Richland Chapel) be re-accepted by the Association.

78th session 1921 - Midway Church, Royal Chapel Church and Emanuel Church be accepted into the

Association.

80th session 1923 - West Nashville Church was accepted into the Association.
There were 32 churches in the Cumberland Association in 1923.

81st session 1924 - East Nashville Free Will Baptist Workers, having as its object the building of a Free Will Baptist Church in East Nashville, rented a hall and began services on September 7th of this year, with Brother Wm. Henry Oliver acting as pastor. A Sunday School was organized with eighteen members and an average Attendance of forty-five at preaching services. It is our plan to organize a church at an early date.

82nd session 1925 - Ashland City, Gorman and West Nashville churches were received into the Association.

86th session 1930 – Association Churches in 1930: Ashland City, Bethel, Bethlehem, Brandon's Chapel, Cofer's Chapel, Craigfield, Dunbar's Chapel, East Nashville, Emanuel's Chapel, Fredonia, Good Springs, Gorman, Head's, Miller's Chapel, Mt. Pleasant, Mt. Zion, New Hope, Oak Grove, Oakland, Oaklawn, Oakwood, Olivet, Pleasant Hill, Rock Springs, Royal Chapel, Scott's Chapel, Shady Grove, Spring Hill, Stoney Point and West Nashville.

89th session 1932 - Motion made and passed to change the name of Royal Chapel in Columbia to the First Free Will Baptist Church.

90th session 1933 - New churches received into the Association
- Hagewood's Chapel at Fredonia.
- Starkey's Chapel in Williamson County.
- Friendship Church in Cheatham County.

94th session 1937 - Petition received from Pewitt's Chapel Church asking admittance into this Association.

107th session 1950 - Request of the First Free Will Baptist Church, Owensboro, KY for membership in this body be granted.

110th session 1953 - New church petitions:
Loyal Chapel Church, Columbia, TN
Mt. Pleasant Church, Mt. Pleasant, TN
Dickson Church, Dickson, TN

111th session 1954 – Association churches in 1954: Ashland City, Barren Plains, Bethel, Bethlehem, Brandon's Chapel, Claude's Chapel, Cofer's Chapel, Columbia First Church, Dickson First Church, Dunbar's Chapel, East Nashville, Friendship, Good Springs, Forman, Head's, Hurricane Chapel, Loyal Chapel, Miller's Chapel, Mt. Pleasant, Mt. Zion, New Hope, New Macedonia, Oak Grove, Oakland, Oaklawn, Oak Wood, Olivet, Owensboro First Church, Pleasant Hill, Pleasant Ridge, Rock Springs, Scott's Chapel, Shady Grove, Springfield First Church, Stony Point, Sylvan Park, Trinity, Union Hill, West Nashville, West Side, and Woodbine.

117th session 1960 - List of churches and Pastors: Ashland City – Joe Hurst, Bethel – Stanley Outlaw,

Bethlehem – Gerald Mangham, Brandon's Chapel – Gene Anderson, Carlisle – H.C. Beasley, Cofer's Chapel – J.L. Welch, Columbia, First – Wallace Paul, Dickson, First – C.A. Craft, Donelson – Francis Boyles, Dunbar's Chapel – Carl Wilson, East Nashville – Dale Burden, East (KY) – Basel Embry, Faith – J.W. Love, Friendship – Fred Warner, Good Springs – David Joslin, Gorman – D.A. Hatcher, Greenwood – Frank Dunn, Heads– Bill Robinson, Horton Heights – Joe Haas, Hurricane Chapel – Jerry Lankford, Layne's Chapel – Walter Layne, Loyal Chapel – W.B. Hughes, Madison – J.L. McIntosh, Manchester – WB. Rogers, Miller's Chapel – O.S. Carroll, Mt. Pleasant – J.J. Abernathy, Mt. Zion – Dean Dobbs, New Hope – John Vick, New Macedonia – J.L. Parsons, Oak Grove – John Warren, Oakland – Luther Reed, Oaklawn – Thomas Johnson, Oakwood (Cedar Hill) – Bobby King, Oak Wood (Woodlawn) Eunis Crowe, Olivet – Fred Hawkins, Owensboro (KY) – {without a pastor}, Pardue Memorial – Charles Jennettee, Pleasant Hill – Billy Jackson, Pleasant Ridge – Don Pegram, Portland – John B. Lindsley, Richland – D.L. Sharp, Rock Springs – James V. Smith, Scott's Chapel – Shelvie Henry, Shady Grove – Bob Ketchum, Springfield – J.B. Parsons, Stony Point – E.M. Grubbs, Sylvan Park – E.A. Craft, Trinity – Robert C. Hill, Union Hill – Ronald Howland, West End (Springfield) – Frank Gunta, West Nashville – Sidney Henry, Woodbine – Douglas Roberson.

120th session 1963 – Harper Road church was received by vote as a new church in the Association.

A current 2018 listing of the pastors and churches at the time of the printing of this book is located in the chapter containing the minutes from the 174th, 2017

Session of the Cumberland Association of Free Will Baptists.

Fulfilling the Great Commission

By
Roy W. Harris

The Cumberland Association throughout its history has been a nationally and internationally forward-thinking organization. Its support for missions, as referred to many times in the minutes, was strong and consistent.

Missions were first mentioned in the 36th session minutes in 1879: *Each church take up one public offering during the year for missions, to be brought to Association for dispersal*.

The Association at the 43rd session seven years later in 1886 recommended *that: Pastors having the care of churches take up four public collections during the ensuing year and funds be sent to the annual meeting of the Association to be placed in the hands of the Mission Board*.

The Cumberland proclaimed its strong belief in *both home and foreign missions* in 1903 during the 53rd session when they stated: *We, as an association, favor missions, both home and foreign*.

The first recorded missionary outreach of the Cumberland Association was the election of Reverend W.M. Rogers as Missionary Preacher at the 60th session in 1903. The role of the Missionary Preacher was defined as follows: *The Missionary Preacher will go where he deems necessary, and preach and do all good in his power for the promotion of God's cause and the salvation of souls. He is instructed to take up collections at his points of preaching and report the same to the next annual session of the Cumberland Association.*

Nine years later at the 69th session in 1912, the Association passed a motion to: *Finish getting up funds to buy a tent for this Association to be used by the Home Missionary.*

The Association appointed its first Home Mission Board in 1914 at the 74th session and voted to keep a Home Missionary in the field. Voted: *We keep a Home Missionary in the field and a Home Mission Board consisting of five members be appointed.*

A suggested plan of support for Home Missions appears two years later in the minutes: *Each church be required to pay 20 cents per member for the cause of Home Missions.*

The Home Mission Board made a motion at the 74th session in 1917 *that: $25 be given to Brother Pickle to help buy a buggy for him.* A Home Mission and Church Extension Fund had been established with a beginning balance of $249.95 and the total with gifts left an ending balance of $428.14.

The formation of the National Association of Free Will Baptists in 1935 ushered in a new era in missions outreach. The Cumberland Association once again became a leader in carrying out the Great Commission to carry the Gospel to Jerusalem, Judea and the uttermost parts of the world.

The Association quickly embraced the newly formed National Association and rallied support for Foreign Missions and Home Missions outreach.

Foreign Missions

A motion was made at the 93rd session in 1937 to

adopt the recommendation of the Free Will Baptist Foreign Mission Board: *That Reverend Thomas Willey be sent to Central or South America to open up a mission field in the name of our Master and the FWB denomination.*

The Association recommended at the 104th session in 1947 that: *Each church sponsor a study course of Miss Barnard's book* His Name Among All Nations, *this be left to the local church as to how it may be carried out.*

114th session in 1957 – Brother Dave Franks, missionary candidate to Brazil, brought a missionary message and gave information for a Free Will Baptist work there.

J.B. Fletcher and Jack Paramore were mentioned as having been elected to the National Foreign Missions Board.

Reverend Rolla Smith reported on the National Foreign Missions work at the 118th session in 1961.

Reverend Norman Richards was mentioned during the 122nd session in 1965 as serving on the National Foreign Missions Board.

The 123rd session in 1966 Recommended that churches keep every family on the mailing list for Heartbeat, the Foreign Missions publication.

Reverend Rolla Smith, director of the Free Will Baptist National Home Missions, spoke for his department at the 132nd session in 1975.

Missionary Allen Crowson gave the Foreign Missions report during the 138th session in 1981.

Missionary Donnie McDonald dismissed the 142nd session in 1985 morning worship service in prayer.

144th session, 1987 – Brother Raymond Riggs introduced his son Steve Riggs, missionary to France, who delivered the Tuesday morning message.

146th session, 1989 – Norman Richards, missionary to Africa, brought the morning message from the Isaiah 6:1-13.

158th session, 2001 – Bobby Pool, missionary to Brazil, brought the 11:00 a.m. message from Luke 14:15-24.

163rd session, 2006 - Brother James Forlines gave the report for Free Will Baptist International Missions.

166th session, 2009 - Brother Barry Simpson gave greetings from the International Missions Department. He thanked the body for their giving. He made a special thank you to Brother Bob Baggett and the Western Quarterly for their work on the Don and Billie Sexton Missions Project.

168th session 2011 – Brother Sam McVay and Dr. David Outlaw spoke on behalf of International Missions. McVay brought greetings from the missionaries and the missions office. He informed the body of the *new* International Missions Director, Brother Clint Morgan.

170th session 2013 – Brother Donnie McDonald

brought greetings from Japan. The McDonalds have been in Japan since 1986. There are three Free Will Baptist Churches in Tokyo.

Brother Henry VanKlyve spoke on the World Mission Offering.

171st session 2014 – Daniel and Katie Speers gave greetings and shared their plans for ministry in Japan. Katie shared her background in Japanese Missions. Japan is an affluent country, but very destitute. They will minister in Tokyo.

Sister Alyssa Harvey expressed appreciation for the support of Cumberland Association for their ministry in China through ELIC. She explained their ministry in China. They are home for a year to raise support for their ministry.

172nd session 2015 – Brother Sam McVay brought greetings from the Free Will Baptist International Missions. Anna Forlines, from Cross Timbers, is currently serving in France. God is opening doors and blessing the work.

173rd session 2016 - Sister Shannon Little brought greetings from the International Missions work in Japan. She thanked the Cumberland Association for the impact it had on her life and ministry. She currently needs $15,000 to be able to return to the mission field.

Free Will Baptist International Missions

Dear Friends of the Cumberland Association,

What a wonderful and rich history you have. Obviously, none present today were there 175 years ago when the Association was established. However, the Cumberland lives on and its influence is wide spread.

From generation to generation the Word of God and a high level of commitment has directed the leaders of the Cumberland to pursue actions that expand His Kingdom. The faithfulness of these godly men and women has set a pattern that has established a solid foundation for the past and will take us into the future.

Through the years you have ordained pastors, commissioned missionaries, championed causes that guaranteed the spread of the gospel and safeguarded the doctrines we hold dearly as Free Will Baptists.

The International Missions family congratulates you for your longevity, 175 years, and honors you for your faithfulness. It is our prayer that you will continue to carry His banner high and be faithful in fulfilling the Great Commission until His return.

Serving Him,

IM

Clint Morgan, General Director

Home Missions

Home Missions has been part of the heartbeat of the Cumberland Association since its beginning. There have been ongoing efforts by the association to begin new churches in Middle Tennessee. The Association quickly embraced the efforts of the National Association in planting churches across North America.

National Home Missions first appears in 1954 at the 111th Cumberland Association meeting: *Reverend Damon Dodd, promotional secretary for the National Home Mission Board spoke on behalf of his work.*

The 118th session minutes in 1961 stated that: *Reverend Homer Willis reported on the work of National Home Missions.*

Reverend Bob Shockey gave the National Home Missions report at the 131st session in 1974.

Director Roy Thomas reported 38 Missionaries in North America. 10 states in America now have Free Will Baptist Churches at the 133rd session in 1976.

Trymon Messer brought greetings from National Home Missions the afternoon business session at the 149th session in 1992.

Glenn Thomas gave a report for National Home Missions at the 150th session in 1993.

Brother Tim McDonald introduced Brother Luis Felipe, Moderator of the Mexican Association during the

171st session in 2014. He thanked the body for sending missionaries (Howard and James Munsey) to Mexico. There are fifty churches in Mexico: *Free Will Baptists have a presence in eight of the states in Mexico. The Bible is being translated into the various Mexican dialects. The Mexican Association has a Children's Home and Bible Institute.*

Brother Clayton Hampton presented his mission work in Montana during the 174th session in 2017: *He has started his itinerary. He asked to be allowed to present at our churches. Please keep this work in your prayers.*

Advocates for Education

By

Roy W. Harris

Free Will Baptists in Middle Tennessee have a long history of advocating for a well-educated presbytery. The Cumberland Association realized the need for training among its ministers as early as 1876.

Sunday Schools as we call them today were first recommended to Middle Tennessee Free Will Baptist churches at that same session and a further recommendation during the following session in 1877:

This Association recommends to all the churches to organize Sabbath Schools, and to get such literature as will be necessary for the students. We deem Sabbath Schools to be an auxiliary of the Church, and we recommend that every Church should organize Sabbath Schools.

The leaders of the Association were men and women of vision who recognized the need for a trained presbytery. This statement by the *Education Committee* found in the 66th session, 1909 Cumberland minutes demonstrates the desperate need for and the strong desire by the Association to encourage an educated presbytery:

It is a deplorable fact that our ministers are far deficient in their educational qualifications compared to other denominations. We earnestly request the Association admonish all candidates for Gospel ministry that they make every effort to obtain an English education. We suggest that the churches assist worthy men in their efforts along these lines, and that individual lay members help such young men and that they secure the cooperation of other churches, in order that the standard of education in our ministerial ranks be raised to its proper place (Education Committee – W.M. Brumit, G.T. Harris, G.E. Gower)

During the 73rd session in 1916, the Education Committee recommended to the Association that a literary standard be adopted for all candidates for the ministry.

Recommended that: *There be a literary standard adopted for candidates for the ministry in this Association, and that all candidates for the ministry in the future be required to measure up to said standard before they shall be ordained to the full work of the ministry.*

That all ordained ministers under the age of 60 years be required to do certain Bible study that shall be outlined at the present sitting of this Association by a committee to be appointed by the moderator.

They also realized that educational opportunities among Free Will Baptists were very limited. They investigated reputable institutions of higher learning and sought to guide and encourage Associational ministers to take advantage of these educational opportunities.

Below is a sampling of the Association's recommendations:
- *Free Will Baptist Theological Institute* of Ridgeville, Indiana (1876, 77, 1885)
- We recommend *Hillsdale College-Michigan- A FWB Institution)* to any young man who desires an education in theology. (1885)
- *The Free Will Baptist Seminary at Ayden, N.C.* is a school worthy of our support. (1900, 1920)
- *First ministers course by mail, (correspondence*

course) developed by Reverend John Wolfe of *Tecumseh, OK* – recommended that all our ministers, especially the young men take advantage of this opportunity. (1919)
- We favor the work of the *Moody Bible Institute* of Chicago, Illinois, for our ministers and that the Association make arrangements for their expenses and their applying to the Chairman of the Executive Committee. (1919)
- Thos E. Beaman made a very interesting talk on Eureka College, Ayden, NC. Association approved Eureka College to be supported and encourage our young people to attend. The Association will elect an *Associate Trustee* to represent the Association. (1927)

The Association offered educational opportunities for ministers and laity from within the Association.

Following is a strong statement in 1912 deploring the educationally deficient candidates seeking to become ministers:

The Education Committee recommended that the Association establish a school for our Ministers to be held annually at a church selected by President of said school; churches are to solicit the President for the privilege of entertaining the School. Reverend J.L. Welch was elected President of the school.

First session would last for one week. Bethlehem Church, Cheatham County was selected. Heads Church, Bethel Church, and Oak Lawn will be the location for the next three sessions.

A motion was made and passed during the 72nd 1920 session, that *Free Will Baptist Leagues* be organized in all our churches for the training of our young people.

The Free Will Baptist League was permitted to insert a report into the 80th 1923 session minutes.

Miss Rebecca Stewart was first mentioned during the 96th session in 1939 and appointed as Chairman of the League Committee..

The Association approved a plan for a *Christian Workers Institute* during the 81st 1924 session. A committee was appointed to arrange for time and program for the Institute:

Upon the suggestion of Reverend J.L. Welch during the 87th 1930 session, the Association voted to begin an Institute in the Cumberland Association and to start in the latter part of this year. The Association voted to hold the Institute at East Nashville Church

Reverend J.L. Welch was elected director of the Institute. Reverend Henry Oliver was elected assistant director:

The Institute began in January of 1932 instead of December 1931 and lasted for one week for study of the most pressing needs of our work. The session was not largely attended, but some good was accomplished among those present. In the courses of study we took up Homiletics, Sunday Schools, Leagues, Ladies Aid, Church Administration, Music and Helps in English.

Free Will Baptist Bible College

The newly formed National Association of Free Will Baptists' Board of Education immediately started developing plans in 1936 to begin a National College.

J.L. Welch, pastor of Cofer's Chapel Free Will Baptist Church and a member of the Cumberland Association had been elected Chairman of the Board of Education.

Plans had been laid to begin the new college in 1936, but we know that it didn't begin until 1942.

North Carolina, with its large number of churches and strong state association, pushed hard for the college to be located there. Weaverville, NC was argued as the consensus location for a number of reasons. Nashville, Tennessee was eventually selected for the location of the national college. The name Free Will Baptist Bible College was chosen.

The Cumberland Association played a huge role in the selection of Nashville for the location of the Free Will Baptist Bible College. The Association had a long track record of a vision for and promotion of higher Christian education. Brother Welch's wisdom, skill, art of persuasion and zeal in large part is responsible for the location of Free Will Baptist Bible College in Nashville, Tennessee.

The 93rd session in 1936 passed a strong resolution that eventually was sent to the National Association of Free Will Baptists Board of Education and the Free Will Baptist paper at Ayden, NC:

Resolution of School of Nashville – We, Ministers, Deacons, and Delegates composing this the 93rd session of the Cumberland Association of Free Will Baptist Churches, do hereby express our appreciation of the untiring efforts of Reverend J.L. Welch to create both a sentiment for and to locate a denominational school at Nashville, TN. While we are willing to trust the wisdom of our educational board, who appear to favor a location at Weaverville, NC, We desire to go on record as favoring the location of same at Nashville, TN. And commend the zeal and persistence of Reverend J.L. Welch in his efforts to have it located there.

On motion and duly second a copy of the above resolution was voted to be sent to the Free Will Baptist paper at Ayden, NC.

The decision was made to locate the new national College in Nashville, Tennessee. Free Will Baptist Bible College opened her doors in September 1942.

The impact of the Cumberland Association is recognized in the fact that the first Association to receive a report from the National College was the Cumberland Association one month later in October 1942.

Reverend Henry Melvin reported the opening of our new school in Nashville, TN, as he described it in the minutes of the 96th session in 1939.

99th session 1942 – National College (Free Will Baptist Bible College):

Reverend Henry Melvin spoke of the National Conference and the opening of our new school in Nashville, TN that has been bought and paid for and is ours now. This school is owned by the Free Will Baptists and is something we should feel proud of. The school is located at 3609 Richland Ave, Nashville, TN.

Motion made and passed to pay out of the Education fund not to exceed $225 for a stove for the kitchen for the National Bible School.

The first meals served in the new college were cooked on the stove paid for by the Cumberland Association.

This began a long and lasting relationship of support for the college by the Association. Below are several people, events, interesting facts, reports etc. that have taken place over the past 75 plus years listed in the minutes. Most of the information below is quoted directly from the minutes.

101ˢᵗ session 1944 - Thursday morning session, *Reverend L.R. Ennis, President of Free Will Baptist Bible College, Mrs. Sawyer, a member of the faculty, and several of the students from the College were recognized.*

103ʳᵈ session 1946 - Reverend L.R. Ennis reported that *fifty-four students* are enrolled in the college at present and *thirteen states* are represented.

105ᵗʰ session 1948: *Reverend Henry Melvin, Business Manager of the College and also Executive Secretary of the National Association who spoke on the national program and also gave a very encouraging report of the Bible College in which he stated that the College now has a Student Body of 73 students. He also emphasized the urgency of expansion at the College.*
In response to Brother Melvin's suggestion that the churches composing the Cumberland Association buy a station wagon for the college; after discussion, a motion was made and sustained that this Association approve the suggestion Brother Melvin mentioned.

106ᵗʰ session 1949: *Since we have in our midst the Reverend Benito Rodriguez from our Cuban School of Missions in Cuba, now enrolled as a student of Free Will Baptist Bible College, and feeling that it is our responsibility to help support him. Be it resolved that this Association request each church of the Cumberland Association to make a monthly contribution to the college to help defray his expenses.*

108ᵗʰ session 1951 - Reverend J.L. Welch, Chairman of the Board of Directors of Free Will Baptist Bible College gave a brief report of the present facilities of the school.

113th session 1956 - The College is beginning its fifteenth year with 171 Students.

119th session 1962 - Reverend Paul Ketteman, representative from the Bible College thanked the Association for its increased support and reported the work of the school.

133rd session 1976 - FWBBC – Dr. L.C. Johnson reported there were 562 students with 175 studying for the ministry.

135th session 1978 - FWBBC – Reverend Ronald Creech reported that last year 640 students were in enrolled at FWBBC.

138th session 1981 - Reverend Frank Breeden gave the report from the Bible College.

146th session 1989 – Ronald Creech asked for prayer for the Bible College Board of Trustees as they look for a new President.

147th session 1990 – Dr. Tom Malone, new President of Free Will Baptist Bible College, brought greetings during the afternoon session.

156th session 1999 - Dr. James Cox, Director of Institutional Effectiveness at FWBBC, brought the 11:00 a.m. message from Hebrews 9:24.

159th session 2002 – Matthew Pinson, new President of Free Will Baptist Bible College, gave a report on the college. Frank Owens gave a report on the College Alumni Project.

160th session 2003 – David Williford reported that: 20% of students and 17% of the financial support the college receives comes from the Cumberland Association.

161st session 2004 – Terry Forrest gave a report about Free Will Baptist Bible College.

163rd session 2006 – David Williford gave the report from Free Will Baptist Bible College.

165th session 2008 - Brother Matt Pinson gave the report from the Free Will Baptist Bible College. He thanked the Cumberland Association for its unparalleled support.

166th session 2009 - Brother Bert Tippett brought greetings from Free Will Baptist Bible College. 302 students enrolled for the fall 2009 semester.

167th session 2010 - Brother Matt Pinson brought greetings from Free Will Baptist Bible College and stated: *The Cumberland Association gives more support to the college than any other association in the National Association.*

168th session 2011 - Dr. Stanley Outlaw brought greetings from Free Will Baptist Bible College. He testified of the impact of the college on his life. The college appreciates the support and relationship it has with the

Cumberland Association.

169th session 2012 - Brother Earl Langley brought greetings from Welch College (first report since the name was changed from Free Will Baptist Bible College to Welch College.) Langley gave his background in the Cumberland Association. He informed the body that there are copies of the college's Annual Report out on the table. *Tennessee is the greatest source of finances and students for the college.* The name change was confirmed at the National Association in July.

170th session 2013 - Brother Earl Langley spoke for Welch College. He reported that enrollment is up, a new four-year online Bible degree is available and the possible sale of the current campus to Aquinas College.

172nd session 2015 - Brother Earl Langley brought greetings from Welch College. The college is moving forward with the location of the campus. The middle Tennessee alumni met at the location of the new campus for a picnic; over 300 attended. The college is moving ahead with the Master of Arts (M.A.) degree in Theology and Ministry.

173rd session 2016 – Brother Mike Edwards gave the Welch College report. He thanked the churches for their support of the college through prayers, finances, and students. Brother Jeff Cockrell brought greetings from the Master's program. There are currently 19 enrolled in the program. The classes are a hybrid study. It is a 33-hour program with ten classes that can be finished in 15 months. Dr. Roy Harris encouraged the body to pray for the college.

174th session 2017 – Dr. Matthew Pinson thanked the Association for its many years of support for Welch College. He also brought a message celebrating the 500th anniversary of the beginning of the Protestant Reformation.

The Cumberland Association has a long-standing relationship with Welch College. Its support for the college has been strong, steadfast and unwavering. It continues to be the number one supporting association among Free Will Baptists.

The Women of the Cumberland

By

Phillip T. Morgan

A Garland of Grace and Crown of Beauty: The Founding and Influence of the Cumberland District Ladies Aid Society

The Cumberland District Women Active for Christ serves as a sister organization to the Cumberland Association. Founded in 1920, this arm of the association is dedicated to the spiritual maturation of Free Will Baptist women and to supporting the missions of the church. Few Free Will Baptist organizations have had as significant an influence on the broader denomination as this group of women.

Led by such luminaries as Fannie Polston (1881-1964), Mary Ann Welch (1890-1969), and Agnes Frazier (1897-1993), the CDWAC was one of the earliest organization for women's work among modern Free Will Baptists. These women developed much of what would eventually become the mission and purpose of the national women's organization. Their concern for spiritual development, stewardship, missions and education would spread far beyond their local district.

Early Women's Ministry in the Cumberland Association

The first efforts toward developing a women's organization within churches now associated with the

National Association of Free Will Baptists (NAFWB) began just before 1900. The earliest records that we have found show a women's "organization in the church at Glennville, Georgia, in 1899."[xliii] Soon thereafter, women's organizations also appeared in North Carolina and Tennessee. Both of these groups have clear ties to the more conservative elements in the Randall Movement of Freewill Baptists.[xliv]

  A West Virginia minister in the Randall Movement named Dell Upton came to Nashville in 1907 to serve as the pastor of Cofer's Chapel Free Will Baptist Church. Mr. Upton was extremely influential even though he remained in Nashville for only two years.[2] Importantly, he introduced the idea of an independent women's ministry that would support the church's mission. On December 17, 1907, the first meeting of the Cofer's Chapel Ladies Aid Society met in his home.[xlv] Both married and single women were welcomed to take part in the group. This organization was designed to include women in building the kingdom of God by providing new opportunities for them to use their talents.

  Two of the founding members of the Cofer's Chapel society were especially important for the later development of women's work throughout the denomination Fannie Polston and Mary Ann Weaver (later Mary Ann Welch). Polston was from Cheatham County, Tennessee, but after she married a pastry chef named Fred Polston in 1902 she moved to Nashville and joined Cofer's Chapel. In *Sparks into Flame*, Mary Ruth Wisehart noted Polston's good

---

[2] Due to the nature of this chapter, when a last name is used to refer to an individual whose spouse is also mentioned, that name will always refer to the wife. Men will be referred to by their titles and sir names.

business sense, intelligence, and courage.[xlvi] These three qualities gave Polston an entrepreneurial character that uniquely suited her for leadership.

Nine years younger than Polston, Mary Ann Weaver and her future husband John L. Welch (1889-1983) best caught the broader vision of Mr. Upton. After the Welches married in 1912, they worked as a team to encourage the formation of a national denomination and a centrally located denominational college. Their diligent promotion of these causes was instrumental in the eventual development of the National Association of Free Will Baptists and Free Will Baptist Bible College (now Welch College). However, they were also committed to growing women's organizations in local churches throughout the denomination.

The Founding of the Cumberland Ladies Aid Societies

Under the encouragement of Mr. Upton, the Cofer's Chapel Ladies Aid Society began publishing a newspaper, *The Free Will Baptist Record*, in 1907. Polston served as the first editor of the paper. Weaver wrote articles and later served as the second editor. *The Record* related the goals and activities of the Ladies Aid, hoping to encourage other churches to begin similar organizations. They wrote about their support for the ministries of the local church, explaining how they raised money and built excitement for special offerings and initiatives like education. After the Ladies Aid had been active for several years and refined its ministry, the paper also focused on stewardship and missions.[xlvii]

Through *The Record* and the work of the Welches, the Cofer's Chapel Ladies Aid was successful in expanding women's work in area Free Will Baptist churches that made up the Cumberland Association. After Mr. Upton returned to West Virginia, Mr. Welch became the minister at Cofer's. Mr. Welch and his new wife Mary Ann actively encouraged building women's organizations in other churches.

Heads Free Will Baptist Church in Turnersville and Rock Springs Free Will Baptist Church in Neptune both formed Ladies Aid Societies in 1916.[xlviii] Oaklawn Free Will Baptist Church in Thomasville and an unknown number of other churches also had active Ladies Aid Societies by 1917. It is unclear how many of these organizations were started through the influence of the Welches and *The Record*. However, the secretary of the Heads Ladies Aid specifically credited the formation of their group to the encouragement of Mr. Welch.[xlix]

Until 1920, these societies remained individual entities connected to the local church. They often sent reports to the annual meeting of the Cumberland Association, but otherwise carried out their activities independent of one another. That year they formed the Ladies Aid Societies of the Freewill Baptists of Tennessee (State Convention). Despite describing themselves as a state organization, this group didn't include any societies outside of the Cumberland Association.

The new organization was both more independent from the Cumberland Association and more involved in their activities. At the 1921 Cumberland meeting, Mrs. J. E. Hudgens reported on the first annual session of the State Convention that had been held a month earlier in September. In addition, she requested "friendly relations" with the Cumberland and welcomed "any suggestions or assistance" the association might have for "the development of our spiritual and material resources."[l] When Hudgens closed her report, she invited their continued correspondence and reassured the body that "we remain Fraternally Yours."[li] This report shows that while the new organization was independent of the Cumberland, they still sought to maintain a close relationship.

    The number of male attendees to the early State Convention meetings highlights the "fraternal" nature of the relationship. Local pastors seemed to have been regular attendees at the meetings and were often invited to share a sermon or lead in prayer. D. T. Armstrong, W. B. Davenport, J. E. Hudgens, William H. Oliver and John L. Welch were often present and active in meetings. In fact, when D. T. Armstrong died, the 1928 obituary committee of the State Convention even referred to him as a member of the organization.[lii] In 1925, the State Convention also approved of a motion to have the Executive Committee appoint a man to promote the work of the societies.[liii] Women remained the leaders of the organization and seemed to welcome the involvement of these men as an act of encouragement and support.

    The independence of the State Convention brought another interesting change. Previously, each local society reported their activities for the year to the Cumberland Association. They told of the money they had raised and how they had dispersed it. However, the new State Convention went beyond reporting their actions and began recommending initiatives for the entire Cumberland Association to engage. Hudgens explained in her 1921 report that the Convention wanted to found an orphanage and a denominational school or college. However, unlike in previous Ladies Aid reports, she called upon the whole association to join with the women in fulfilling these tasks.[liv]

    Several Cumberland churches pledged to raise

money toward these ends in the coming year. In fact, they pledged to raise the ambitious amount of $15,224.20 (roughly equivalent to $202,000 in 2018).[lv] The Cumberland Association began gathering funds for these initiatives, raising $1,068.70 (roughly equivalent to $16,000 in 2018) by the next annual session.[lvi] This money was used to support students from Cofer's who were attending Ayden Seminary in North Carolina that year and to pay John H. Oliver for a school (probably a short Christian education training session) he led in Dover that year.[lvii] These goals eventually were met in the founding of the Children's Home in Greeneville, Tennessee, and Free Will Baptist Bible College.

Soon after the State Convention was formed, more Tennessee Free Will Baptist churches developed women's organizations. The Union Association of Ladies Aids began holding annual meetings in 1927 under a similar name to the Cumberland women: the Convention of the Ladies' Aid Society of Free Will Baptists of Tennessee. With multiple associations in the state, it became necessary to differentiate between the groups. Therefore, in 1929, the women of the Cumberland Association renamed their organization the Cumberland District Ladies Aid Societies (CDLAS),[3] and the women of the Union Association followed suit in 1931, renaming their group the Union Association Ladies Aid Societies.[lviii] By the time the State Convention became the CDLAS, it could boast twenty-five societies in its membership.[lix] The faithful work of those first women in the Upton home was paying dividends.

---

[3] The CDLAS made several modifications to its title during the twentieth century. The name Cumberland District Women Active for Christ was likely adopted in 1994 (the minutes for 1992 and 1993 are missing).

The Mission of the Cumberland Ladies Aid Societies

In the early years of women's work among Free Will Baptists, there was little cohesion to their mission or goals. As late as the early 1920s, many of these organizations thought of themselves as "little group[s] banded together to carry out [their] own separate programs."[lx] Most focused on needs in the local church, such as providing new furnishings or paying the minister. But this attitude soon changed under the leadership of Polston who served as the CDLAS president from 1926-1929. According to her, these organizations had become active participants in the broader mission of the church by the early 1930s.[lxi] The CDLAS tried to build-up the church's ministries in spiritual development, stewardship, missions, and education.[lxii]

The societies promoted spiritual development through study and prayer. Each meeting of the societies was supposed to include a Bible lesson that was meant to encourage further study. Polston also wanted to emphasize prayer, so in 1930 she developed an annual week of prayer for the Cumberland societies to observe in November.[lxiii] In addition, some societies studied books on Christian discipline. In 1929, Polston reported that the CDLAS had studied Charles A. Cook's book on "Stewardship and Missions."[lxiv] Later she recommended Cook's *The Larger Stewardship"* and Helen Barrett's *Prayer and Mission*.[lxv] These books were soon applied to the goals of the Ladies Aid societies.

Stewardship became a special emphasis of the Cumberland societies through the work of another early leader, Agnes Frazier. Frazier attended Bethlehem Free Will Baptist Church in Ashland City during her childhood. After marrying in 1917, Frazier moved to Alabama before ending up in Nashville around 1925. She and her husband James joined East Nashville Free Will Baptist Church which had recently been gathered through the work of Polston and the Welches.

The Welches strongly encouraged Frazier, a school teacher, to begin writing material for Ladies Aid societies to use in their monthly meetings. In 1929, Frazier responded by writing her first pamphlet entitled *Stewardship and Missions*. Before meeting the Welches, Frazier did not remember ever hearing about tithing or stewardship.[lxvi] However, through their ministry she became convinced that Christ has dominion over more than ten percent of a person's income.

In 1931, the women at the annual session of the CDLAS elected Frazier the superintendent of stewardship and missions, replacing Welch. Later this position was restructured to focus on stewardship alone. When the societies first formed in the early 1900s, they focused their efforts on raising money for special projects through community fundraisers. Through the work of Frazier and before her Welch, most Cumberland District societies started practicing regular financial giving above their tithe. Beyond this regular giving, they continued to raise funds through quilt sales, bake sales and other public events. As a result, the societies began raising a significant amount of money.

Much of the money raised by these societies went to missions. The women of the Cumberland began to advocate for foreign missions work well before any modern Free Will Baptist missionary had actually entered the field. Mrs. Miles Gower from Heads Church served as the chairwoman of missions in 1928 and reported that nine churches had held missions services in the previous year.[lxvii] Welch, in her 1929 report as the superintendent of stewardship and missions, called the women of the Cumberland to pray for people to understand that stewardship was essential for supporting missions.[lxviii] Making clear the import of her argument, Welch then argued that without missions Christianity was a "hollow mockery."[lxix]

    The other important emphasis for financial support was education. One of the goals of the monthly meetings was to provide Bible education for women who would otherwise have no access to it. Beyond this, the women of the Cumberland District were interested in a Free Will Baptist college. One of the utmost goals for *The Record* all the way back in 1908 had been to raise support for a Free Will Baptist institution in Nashville. Polston's interest in education eventually earned her a seat on the board of Eureka College, a Free Will Baptist institution in Ayden, North Carolina.[lxx]

    Frazier and the Welches' daughter Jean both spoke persuasively about the cause of a Free Will Baptist college at the 1938 annual session of the Cumberland Association. These speeches led to Frazier publishing multiple articles on behalf of the Board of Education for the National Association of Free Will Baptists to raise support for a denominational college and **Jean Welch** making her plea before the 1939 annual session of the National Association. The women of the CDLAS also gave financial support to Eureka College, Zion Bible School in Blakely, Georgia, and eventually Free Will Baptist Bible College (now Welch College).[lxxi]

    This concern for education was also manifested in the CDLAS's work to found an orphanage. Interest in working with orphanages first became apparent in 1920. That year the Cofer's Ladies Aid Society reported to the

Cumberland Association that they had "held a shower for the benefit of the Orphanage at Middlesex, N.C., and received clothing and other articles to the amount of fifty dollars" (roughly equivalent to $650.00 in 2018).[lxxii] The next year at the first annual session of the State Convention (soon to be renamed the CDLAS) on September 28, 1921, the women adopted their own orphanage plans.[lxxiii] A month later they requested that the Cumberland Association join in their work.[lxxiv] The women began looking for a good location for the orphanage, but were unable to find a suitable lot for years. Still, they continued to raise money and by 1926, they had $3,674.27 (roughly equivalent to $52,000 in 2018) on hand for the orphanage.[lxxv]

At the 1938 organizational meeting of the Tennessee State Association of Free Will Baptists, the CDLAS agreed to allow the new state organization to take over their orphanage project. The state association voted to purchase about 160 acres near Greeneville, Tennessee, for $4,500 (roughly equivalent to $80,000 in 2018).[lxxvi] During the second day of the meeting, the state association also named a "Board of Control" for the orphanage that included Mrs. Nancy Parker from the CDLAS as the chairwoman.[lxxvii] It's worth noting that Polston was part of the nominating committee charged with developing this board.[lxxviii]

The CDLAS also advocated for temperance under the aegis of their educational goals. Both Polston and Welch were leaders in the temperance movement in Nashville before the ratification of the XVIII Amendment in 1919. Perhaps because the manufacture, sale and transportation of alcohol was illegal when the CDLAS formed, they did not originally mention temperance at their meetings. However, in 1926 Polston presented a plan to the Executive

Committee of the CDLAS that would instruct each local society to elect a chair who would emphasize certain subjects during the year, one of which was temperance.[lxxix] Welch led the implementation of this plan in 1928 through the Resolutions Committee.[lxxx] This renewed interest was likely founded on larger political movements to repeal the XVIII Amendment. After the ratification of the XXI Amendment in 1933 which repealed the XVIII Amendment, the Temperance Committee ceased to exist. For the next four years, the education committee reported that local societies were still dispersing temperance literature, but after 1937 the temperance movement disappeared from the minutes.

Beyond the Cumberland

As the CDLAS grew, they became leaders beyond the Middle Tennessee area. In the 1920s and 30s the Cumberland ladies helped build interest in Free Will Baptist women's work around the Southeast. When the General Conference and Co-operative General Association began moving toward unification in 1935, CDLAS leaders began developing a national women's movement. Without their influence, the landscape of women's work among Free Will Baptists today would look much different.

The General Conference in the Southeast was first gathered in 1921 by Mr. Welch. Churches from Alabaman, Georgia, North Carolina, and Tennessee sent delegates to that first meeting held at Cofer's Chapel on May 26. For the next seventeen years, the General Conference met annually enriching the common identity of Free Will Baptists and providing an avenue for accountability and mutual support. In 1938, the General Conference ceased to meet in deference to the newly formed NAFWB.

The women of the Cumberland were very active in building a larger women's movement through the General Conference. Polston again showed her leadership as she quickly stepped up to extol the work of the Ladies Aid Societies and encourage the development of new societies. Though it was preferable for a woman to lead the societies, in instances where no woman was willing, Polston recommended having the pastor lead the formation of a society until such a woman could be found.[lxxxi] As a result of her leadership, she was nominated to serve on the first General Conference Ladies Aid Committee formed in 1925.[lxxxii]

When the conference shifted from committees and boards toward general secretaries of departments in 1926, Polston became general secretary of the women's work (a position she held until 1935).[lxxxiii] Polston poured herself into the wider sphere of work afforded her by this position. She immediately began corresponding with women and societies in Alabama, Florida, Georgia, Missouri, Ohio, South Carolina, and West Virginia.[lxxxiv]

Polston also developed a manual in 1927 to be used by Ladies' Aid Societies around the country. The manual's title well describes the book's purpose, *Constitution and By-laws of the State Auxiliary Convention and Its Local Societies*. Polston's manual gave instructions for establishing and carrying out a local, district, and state level women's work, with an overview of the purpose and goals of the organizations, a suggested program guide, and constitution and by-laws for each level of organization.[lxxxv] The General Conference officially adopted the manual in 1927.[lxxxvi]

In preparation for the formation of the National Association of Free Will Baptists, Polston asked for the women in Attendance at the General Conference meeting at Black Jack Church in North Carolina in June 1935 to be dismissed to form the Woman's National Auxiliary Convention (now the Women Nationally Active for Christ).[lxxxvii] A committee of fifteen women from around the denomination had been appointed by the moderator of the General Conference at the request of Polston for the purpose of forming a national organization for women's work among Free Will Baptists. Of that fifteen, three came from the Cumberland Association: Frazier, Polston, and Welch. Serving as chair of the meeting, Polston guided the process of electing the national officers. Frazier presented the plan for organization that was adopted unanimously. This was the same plan she had used to form the CDLAS.[lxxxviii]

      Recognizing Polston's tireless leadership and gifts for communication, the women voted for her to serve as the field secretary, a position she held until 1941.[lxxxix] The first officers of the WNAC also included Welch as first vice president in charge of publications and Frazier as fourth vice president in charge of stewardship.[xc]

      After the founding of the WNAC, the Cumberland women remained influential. Polston continued to guide the development of the organization for the next six years and set an example of excellence for generations of leaders to follow. In 1940, Frazier produced the first WNAC manual and the next year she prepared a book of programs. The WNAC also adopted Frazier's Standard of Achievement program that she had developed for the CDLAS in 1933.[xci] The Standard of Achievement provided incentives for the development of local societies. Frazier, Polston, and Welch continued to be influential leaders for women in the WNAC until their deaths.

Conclusion

Despite their small beginnings in 1907 in a Nashville home, the CDWAC has become one of the most influential Free Will Baptist organizations of the twentieth century. Their commitment to excellence was seen by all as they encouraged spiritual development, stewardship, missions and education. Their constant sacrificial giving to special projects like the orphanage and a denominational college inspired others to join them. As the Free Will Baptists' denomination took on definition in the twentieth century, they were an essential part of building a national women's movement that is still active today. Yet in all things they have sought to bring glory to God rather than themselves. But excellence does not go unnoticed. In an association with a rich heritage and many influential leaders, they have been the garland of grace and crown of beauty.

To the Cumberland Association of Free Will Baptists

Woman Nationally Active for Christ

August 3, 2018

Cumberland Association
Tennessee State Association of Free Will Baptists
Nashville, TN

Dear Friends,

Thank you so much for 175 years of faithful service to the Lord, His Kingdom and Free Will Baptists. Only eternity will reveal the full impact of your ministry.

We are grateful for the contributions made in the earliest years by Cumberland women that so profoundly impacted the formation of WNAC. Ladies of the CDWAC have continuously been the leaders in Tennessee WAC work to the present time. It is exciting to see results in our ministry that had her beginnings here in the Cumberland District Ladies' Aid Society.

Emphases on spiritual growth, stewardship, education, missions, and ministry endeavors continue. These emphases are also important in our FWB international sister organizations that have been influenced by missionaries trained in our FWB colleges. And the harvest continues.

May God continues to bless the Cumberland Association and the CDWAC as you minister now building on the foundation left for you that will be built upon by the next generations. God is faithful.

Serving together until He comes.

Elizabeth

Elizabeth C. Hodges
Director

Publications, Literature and Reading Materials

By

Roy W. Harris

The Cumberland Association's first meeting in 1843 was highlighted with the printing and distributing of a record of the meeting. This was a great beginning and set a precedent for what would follow for the next 175 years.

We owe Brother B.F. Binkley and the Association a debt of gratitude for beginning a yearly record of proceedings that became known as *The Minutes of the Cumberland Association*.

Brother B.F. Binkley was appointed to superintend the printing and distributing the Minutes, and have at least 300 copies struck.

The infant Association recognized the importance of Christian literature and reading materials for its churches. The search began for publishing houses and materials suitable for recommendation to its members.

The Cumberland Association's first recorded recommendation was the *Baptist Review* suggested at the 34th session in 1877.

We recommend the Baptist Review to our brethren, and that every one of them should take it.

The Association's first recommendation of a Free Will Baptist publishing house appears in the 1884, 41st session minutes. *Sabbath School literature may be purchased from the Free Will Baptist Publishing House at Dover, New Hampshire.* (quoted from the minutes)

The 42nd and 43rd sessions minutes from 1885 and 1886 recommended more publishing houses.

42nd session 1885 - *We recommend the literature published by the Free Will Baptist Publishing House at Boston, Massachusetts.*

43rd session 1886 - *We recommend that we adopted the Morning Star, published at Boston, Mass., as our religious organ; also the Free-will Baptist, published at Minneapolis, Minn.*

The need for a denominational publishing house to serve the Cumberland Association and its fellow Free Will Baptist Churches in the *General Association* (later called the *General Conference*) became an early goal for the Cumberland.

47th session 1890 - *We favor heavily the establishment of a denominational Publishing house, to publish* the *Herald and such other publications as our cause demands—all to be under the supervision and control of the General Association.*

The *Association recommended the Harvest Gleaner* published in Georgia four years later in 1894. The Association churches were asked to report the following year the amount of Sunday School work done by them.

The Free Will Baptist published at Ayden, North Carolina was adopted to be used by Cumberland Association Churches at the 54th session in 1887.

We adopt The Free Will Baptist published at Ayden, N.C. as our organ until such time as we shall have and support one of our own.

The Cumberland Association attempted to begin its own publishing house in 1916. The 73rd session Minutes record the following motions that were seconded and passed:
- *To purchase a printing press.*
- *Printing press to be installed at Ashland City, TN.*
- *The deacons of each member church constitute a committee to collect money and with which to purchase a printing press and that they forward the amount received to the clerk.*

David C. Cook literature was recommended to the Association's Sunday Schools in 1924 during he 81st session. *We advise our Superintendents and teachers to investigate the David C. Cook literature for the purpose of obtaining helpful literature that our Publishing Co does not handle.*

C.K. Dunn of Ayden, NC, delegate for the Free Will Baptists of his State, was called on during the 82nd session in 1925 to make a statement in regard to the printing establishment of *Free Will Baptist Publishing Co.* of which institution he is superintendent. He explained that it *was* the official publishing company of the Free Will Baptists of the United States.

The Association voted to purchase two hundred dollars stock in the corporation. One hundred and eighty dollars were subscribed by public donation for this cause.

The relationship with the *Free Will Baptist Press* of Ayden, NC, continued until 1961. The Association was keenly aware of the problems between the old North Carolina Free Will Baptist State churches and the National Association of Free Will Baptists. The following resolution was passed during the 118th Cumberland Association session in 1961:

> *Whereas the Cumberland Association owns 20 shares of stock in the Free Will Baptist Press of Ayden, NC, and whereas this Press is longer cooperating with our National Program: Be it resolved that this association instruct its officers to endeavor to get the money from this stock and donate it to the National Sunday School Board to assist them in launching their new literature program.*

The early 1960s saw the launch of the National Association's Free Will Baptist Sunday School Department. The Cumberland embraced this new publishing house and recommended it to the Association churches. This new Department of the National Association of Free Will Baptists located its home in Nashville, TN, in the heart of the Cumberland Association.

Opposition to Alcohol

By

Roy W. Harris

The Cumberland Association has a long history of opposition to the production and consumption of alcoholic beverages. The Association was very active and influential in the crusade to make prohibition the law of the land.

The *Temperance Committee* was formed and served for over 100 years dealing with not only alcohol but also gambling and other issues deemed detrimental to the church and Christian life in general. Work of the Temperance Committee is also found in other chapters.

A sampling of the Association's stand against alcohol is found below. Most of what is printed are direct quotes from the minutes of the Cumberland Association.

33rd session 1876 - *That we consider the manufacture, sale, and use, as a beverage, of intoxicating liquors, unbecoming a Christian and unsafe in a community, and we advise our brethren to use their influence to prevent either.*

51st session 1894 - *We, the Cumberland Association of Freewill Christian Baptists, in association assembled, in common with other Christian organizations, recommend temperance for the individual, and we as a church, use our influence for the promotion of the temperance cause. We recommend all ministers of this association give special attention to its evils, and that an unceasing effort be made by them to impress these truths upon their hearers.*

54th session 1897 - *That we, the Freewill Baptists, oppose the use of all intoxicants as a beverage; and Whereas millions are sent to perdition by the use of liquor, we recommend that our ministers and laymen advocate and practice total abstinence from all intoxicants.*

56th session 1899 - *The use of fermented and intoxicating liquors are harmful to our influence, destructive to life, and damning to the souls of men. Be it resolved that we as ministers and members will use our influence to destroy, this, the most damning and soul-destroying evil in our land.*

63rd session 1906 - *We lend our aid to all temperance societies and the Anti-Saloon League in their efforts to exterminate the liquor traffic.*

66th session 1909 - *We spare neither vigilance nor means to keep our State in the forward march for National Prohibition.*

67th session 1910 - *Resolved: The Temperance Committee Report encouraged the Cumberland Association to join the effort to take Prohibition beyond the State of TN to make Prohibition the law of the United States.*

70th session 1913 - *Temperance: We as an Association go on record as favoring the abolition of the traffic as a whole, both State and National and especially do we urge the passage of the Anti Jug Law by the United States.*

72nd session 1915 - *Temperance: We urge Congress to submit the Prohibition amendment to the States for their ratification or rejection, and urge upon our people the speedy ratification of this national prohibition amendment.*

73rd session 1916 – *Temperance (Prohibition) We urge Congress (of the United States) to submit the prohibition amendment to the States for their ratification or rejection, and urge upon our people the speedy ratification of this national prohibition amendment.*

Communication with Outside Organizations

By

Roy W. Harris

The Cumberland Association recognized early in its existence the need to communicate with other organizations. The pastors and churches of the Cumberland understood that more could be accomplished for God's Kingdom through joint efforts than it could accomplish alone.

The first recorded communication with an outside organization is found in the 55th 1898 session minutes. The Association instructed Reverend J.E. Hudgens to *bear a letter and fraternal greetings to the Eastern and Western Divisions of the Stone Association of Free Will Baptists.* This began a long and rocky relationship with the Stone Association of Free Will Baptists.

The Association continued its newly established relationship with the Eastern and Western Divisions of the Stone Association and also expanded its horizons five years later. The moderator appointed *corresponding delegates* in the 60th and 61st sessions in 1903 and 1904 to attend and represent the Cumberland Association of Free Will Baptists to the following organizations:

- *Western Division of the Stone Association*
- *General Association of General Baptists*
- *Mt. Union Association of General Baptists*
- *Eastern Division of the Stone Association*

- *Cape Fear Conference of Freewill Baptists of North Carolina.*

The Association continued to reach out to other organizations. A *corresponding letter* from G.W. Frey, President of Geauga and Portage Free Will Baptists of Auburn, Ohio, was read to the body during the 62nd 1905 session. The letter gave some interesting statistics from this group of Ohio Free Will Baptists:
- Five yearly meetings were held.
- 19 quarterly meetings
- 120 churches
- 95 ministers
- 7,633 members
- $181,750 of church property
- Gave $1,500 for Home and Foreign Missions

The Cumberland also received a letter from the *General Conference of Ohio* stating within the Ohio General Conference there were: 1,514 churches, 86,983 members; church property $3,100,033. Paid for Home and Foreign Missions $382,986.01

This was ten years before several northern and northeastern Free Will Baptist Associations from the Randall movement merged with the Northern Baptists in 1910-11.

E.W. Stone from the *Stone Association of Free Will Baptists* brought a letter to the Cumberland Association's 63rd 1906 session from the Stone Association's meeting at Cane Creek Church, Putnam County, TN. A letter was also received from the Western Division of the Stone Association of Free Will Baptists from their session at Shady Grove Church, Putnam County, TN.

The regular order of business was suspended and Elder E.W. Stone of the Stone Association was invited to seat. J.E. Hudgens received him with appropriate words in behalf of the Association.

Delegates were appointed to represent the Cumberland Association to:
- *The Free Baptists of Illinois*
- *General Baptist*
- *Eastern Division of the Stone Association of TN*
- *Cape Fear conference of Freewill Baptist of NC*
- *Ohio Conference*

Contact continued on a variety of fronts. Delegates were appointed in the 71st 1914 session to *correspond with; an Association of Freewill Baptists in Missouri* (name of association not given.) Also, delegates to the *Stone River Association* were appointed.

Reverend O.L. Johnson and Reverend L.O. Roberts of the *General Association of the General Baptists from Oakland City, Indiana*, were invited to sit in council during the 92nd 1935 session of the Cumberland Association. They invited the Cumberland Association to send a delegate to the General Association of General Baptists, which meets at Pool, KY on Tuesday, Wednesday, and Thursday, before the fourth Sunday of October 1935.

Five delegates were appointed to represent the Cumberland Association at the Stone Association and nine delegates appointed to represent at the Free Will Baptist State Association during the 96th session of the Cumberland in 1939.

Dr. Robert Picirilli presented a letter to the body addressed to the Stone Association during the 128th session of the Cumberland in 1971. The letter gave a brief history of the relationship between the two associations and stated that delegates were being sent to the Stone Association to present the letter and try to restore this fellowship.

Motion made, seconded and carried to send the letter and delegates to the Stone Association. Dr. Picirilli, Reverend Richard Cordell and Reverend Herbert Wilkerson were appointed to go as delegates.

The moderator read a letter from the Western Division of the Stone Association during the 129th session of the Cumberland in 1972. He recognized the fraternal delegates: Reverend Jack Taylor and Reverend Burdett Randolph.

Reverend Richard Cordell, Reverend George Ludwig, Reverend Don Lamb, Reverend Carson Whitaker and Reverend J.L. Welch were appointed as fraternal delegates representing the Cumberland Association to the Stone Association.

Reverend Don Worrell brought greetings from the Nashville Union Mission during the 149th session in 1992.

Reverend Leroy Forlines brought greetings from the Baptist believers in Ukraine and Russia during the 153rd session in 1995. He also brought the 11:00 a.m. message from 1 Corinthians 16:9.

The Cumberland Association has a rich history of communicating with and reaching out to other organizations of similar faith and goals. The interactions with outside entities recorded in this chapter are not intended to be exhaustive. Those mentioned above provide a sampling and additional details and contacts are recorded in other places in this book.

General Conference of Free Will Baptists

By

Roy W. Harris

The Cumberland Association voted to seek membership in the General Assembly of Free Will Baptists at the 75th session of the Cumberland in 1918. The Association was accepted as members to the General Conference and agreed to host the 1921 session of the General Conference of Free Will Baptists to be held at Cofer's Chapel Church in Nashville, TN.

The exact wording in the 1920, 77th session minutes states: *We approve of a General Conference of Freewill Baptists to meet with Cofer's Chapel, Nashville, TN on Friday before the fifth Sunday in May 1921. The Moderator appointed delegates to said Conference.*

D.B. Sassor, delegate from the General Conference of North Carolina, made a talk on Educational and Orphanage work during the 79th session.

J.E. Hudgens and D.T. Armstrong were chosen at the 1923 session as delegates to the General Conference of Free Will Baptists to be held in May 1924 in South Carolina.

The Cumberland Association began to play an important role soon after becoming part of the *General Conference of Free Will Baptists.* The 81st session minutes in 1924 states: *Steady progress is being made by the General Conference of Free Will Baptists. Representatives of the Cumberland Association of Tennessee are playing an important part.*

Delegates were elected in the 83rd session in 1926 to the General Conference of Free Will Baptists, which would be meeting at the Salem Church in Florida on the Wednesday before the third Sunday in June 1927.

The 1928 minutes from the 85th session record the States who were represented at the 1928 meeting of the General Conference of Free Will Baptists at Ayden, North Carolina. These were Alabama, Florida, Georgia, North Carolina, Ohio, South Carolina and Tennessee.

W.B. Davenport and G.W. Fambrough were appointed to represent the Association at the General Conference of Free Will Baptists in the State of Georgia in June 1929.

W.B. Davenport and G.W. Fambrough gave a report at the 86th session in October 1929 on the General Conference of Free Will Baptists that met in June 1929 in Glennville, Georgia:

- The Conference met in Glennville, GA, June 12-14 1929. Six states were represented: North Carolina, South Carolina, Georgia, Alabama, Florida and Tennessee. "In all, it was a great advancement for our denomination."
- The Conference will meet next year in Vernon, AL. "We hope to have the western states to join in with us."
- Reverend J.L. Welch, Field Secretary of the General Conference gave us a view to the expansion of our national work.
- Reverend Henry Melvin is mentioned for the first time as having given a report.

J.L. Welch and Fannie Polston were elected at the 88th session in 1931 as delegates to the June 1932 General Conference of Free Will Baptists meeting in Bryon, TX.

J.E. Hudgens and William. H. Oliver were elected at the 89th session in 1932 as delegates to the General Conference meeting in June 1933 at East Nashville Church in Nashville, TN.

Minutes from the 92nd session of the Cumberland Association in 1935 recorded the following report from the Association delegates who attended the June meeting of the General Conference of Free Will Baptists:

The conference was a progressive gathering. The convention adopted the consolidation with the Western Division or Co-Operative Association and now we are one National Conference and this conference will convene in Nashville, TN, on November 5, 1935. We found very progressive people with fine churches.

The moderator appointed J.E. Hudgens and W.J. Paul as delegates to the National Conference historical meeting at Cofer's Chapel Church on November 5, 1935. These two men were also appointed to attend the General Conference at Glennville, GA in June 1936.

National Association of Free Will Baptists

By

Roy W. Harris

The Cumberland Association recognized early that joining with other churches and organizations with like doctrines and beliefs could accomplish more for Christ and His Kingdom. The records indicate the continual seeking of opportunities to partner with others dating back to the 1800s.

The Cumberland Association's influence is readily seen with the formation of the National Association of Free Will Baptists. The historical organizational meeting of what is now the National Association of Free Will Baptists was hosted by Cofer's Chapel Free Will Baptist Church with the strong approval and support of the Cumberland Association of Free Will Baptists.

The Cumberland Association Churches, from the beginning of the National Association in 1935, continue to be near the top in support of National Association departments, agencies, organizations, institutions and programs.

The close relationship between the Cumberland Association and the National Association can be seen throughout the decades. The Cumberland Association minutes record a variety of interactions between the two.

Below is a collection of people, departments, agencies, institutions, reports, general information and etc.

beginning in 1938. They are printed exactly the way they were recorded in the Cumberland Association minutes.

95th session 1938 - Motions made and adopted that: *the Eastern Association of Free Will Baptists endorses and recommends that: Annual meetings of the National Association take place each year. The place of the meeting to alternate each year, east of the Mississippi one year and west of the Mississippi the next year.*

100th session 1943 – Reverend Robert Crawford, National Executive Secretary, gave News from the denominational field.

103rd session 1946 - Reverend R.B. Crawford presented a report of the National Work, which showed a great increase in all departments. The records reveal that there were 2,886 churches reporting to the National Association.

105th session 1948 - *Judging from the requests and discussions coming to the various local and quarterly meetings, now seems to be the time to present and adopt a workable district association program, which, of course, should harmonize with the 1948-49 National Association Program. Therefore, be it resolved that this association adopt for its 1948-49 Plan of Work the following:*
- *Foreign Missions – 30%*
- *Bible College - 30%*
- *Home Missions – 20%*
- *Superannuation – 10%*
- *Home for Children – 10%*

110th session 1953 - Reverend W.S. Mooneyham, Executive Secretary of the National Association brought the morning message – What is a Christian?

120th session 1963 - Reverend Harold Harrison, representing the Sunday School Department of the National Association, spoke on behalf of his work.
Reverend Fred Hall led in singing. The Bible College Choir, led by Donald Clark, presented a short program.

122nd session 1965 - Reverend Ken Riggs National Director of Youth Activities reported on the new Church Training Service work.
The Bible College Choir, led by Director David Randlett, rendered a selection of special numbers in song.

124th session 1967 - Reverend Rufus Coffey gave the report of the National Association.

133rd session 1976 – Reverend Jack Williams gave a report.
Reverend Harold Harrison from the National Sunday School Department reported that the department had distributed 1,600,000 pieces of literature last year.

Reverend Larry Hampton brought greetings from the National CTS Department.

135th session 1978 - Reverend Jack Williams included in his report the merger of the Sunday School and CTS Departments.

144th session 1987- Brother Bill Foster represented the Sunday School Department.

152nd session 1995 - Keith Fletcher brought greetings from Randall House in the afternoon business session.

153rd session 1996 - Bill Evans brought greetings from the Board of Retirement and Insurance and also the Free Will Baptist Foundation.

161st session 2004 - Ray Lewis brought greetings from the Board of Retirement and noted that Director Bill Evans would be retiring in July.

166th session 2009 - Brother Ray Lewis gave greetings from the Board of Retirement. He encouraged those present to get involved in the retirement program.

Free Will Baptist Board of Retirement

Over the 49-year history of the Free Will Baptist Board of Retirement, we have worked hard to help FWB employees prepare for their future ministry. We understand that without help from our FWB churches and Associations this mission would not be accomplished.

The Cumberland Association is one of those associations that has helped further the ministry of our department. Cumberland Association has always supported our ministry by allowing us representation at their meetings and encouraging fellow members of the association to be involved in the retirement program. Cumberland Association also provides financial support through the Together Way Program that helps underwrite some of the operations of Board of Retirement.

We are truly thankful for the ministry provided by the Cumberland Association and pray for their continued success.

Thank you all,

John Brummitt
President and CEO
Board of Retirement
National Association of Free Will Baptist

Tennessee State Association of Free Will Baptists

By
Roy W. Harris

The Cumberland and Union Associations were leaders in forming the Tennessee State Association of Free Will Baptists. This chapter does not give a detailed account of the formation of the Tennessee State Association of Free Will Baptists.

A detailed account of the formation of the Tennessee State Association is available through the State Office. The Tennessee State Association of Free Will Baptists celebrated its 75th anniversary in 2013. The State Office produced a history of the Tennessee State Association that is available upon request. (https://tnfwb.org)

This chapter contains information from the minutes about the Cumberland's interest in and steps taken towards forming a State Association of Tennessee Free Will Baptists.

81st session 1924
- *On motion, the Association approved the efforts being put forth toward forming a State Convention.*
- *J.L. Welch was chosen as our representative in this work.*
- *The Moderator appointed Brother G.T. Harris and Reverend J.H. Oliver to work, advise, and serve with J.L. Welch in this matter.*

88th session 1931 - *Telegram received from Brother J.S. Burgess, Morristown, TN, saying: Get your people ready for State Convention if they desire to unite in this work; if they decide to take part, get a committee of five to be called together at Greenville, please send names and addresses to me, date fixed later.*
- *On a motion, the Chair appointed a committee of five to meet with a committee in Greenville, TN, date to be fixed later to organize a State Convention.*
- *J.L. Welch, W.B. Davenport, W.J. Paul and J.H. Oliver were appointed.*

89th session 1932 - Special Committee Report (The committee was appointed in the 1931 session.)
- *We met with the Union Association of Greenville, TN and organized a State Convention.*
- *The following officers were elected:*
  - *State President – Reverend GEO. D. Dunbar of Chucky, TN*
  - *Secretary - Reverend G.W. Fambrough of Neptune, TN*
  - *Treasurer – J.S. Burgess of Chucky, TN*
- *The new State Convention will meet at Elizabethton, TN, on Thursday before the fourth Sunday in October 1932.*

J.L. WELCH and J.E. HUDGINS were appointed to attend the State Convention.

104th session 1947 - Motion made to send $50 to the State Association as state dues.

125th session 1968 - The Association voted in the 1967 session to begin the publication of a state paper. This has been carried out and The *ECHO* has been circulated to the churches throughout the year.

128th session 1971 - Richard Cordell, State Promotional Secretary for Tennessee gave a report on the state work and projects.

131st session 1974 – *Resolution: Whereas the Tennessee State Association has adopted the Cooperative Plan of Support, and whereas, this plan supports all phases of our state and national work, Therefore, we encourage the churches of the Cumberland Association to adopt the Cooperative Plan of Support.*

140th session 1983 - *Reverend Raymond Riggs, State Promotional Director, gave his report.*

144th session 1987 – *Raymond Riggs, the Promotional Director for the State of Tennessee gave a report and also reminded the association that the 50th Tennessee State Meeting would be held November 9-11, 1987 in Dickson, TN.*

150th session 1993 - *Dr. Charles Thigpen gave greetings from the State Promotional Office and also brought the afternoon message.*

165th session 2008 - *Brother Glenn Poston presented the Tennessee Promotional report. He appreciates the Cumberland Association's activity. He thanked the body for their support of the State work.*

Glenn Poston became State Promotional Director January 1, 2007. He has faithfully attended and reported on the State work at the Cumberland Association annual meetings since that time.

Free Will Baptist Home for Children

By

Roy W. Harris

The Cumberland Association has had a heart for children throughout its history. The relationship between the Association and Free Will Baptist Family Ministries began when the Free Will Baptist Home for Children was started in 1939. Mrs. Fannie Polston was heavily involved along with many others through the years.

Interesting events and actions involving the Cumberland Association and the Children's Home are listed in the minutes below. The minutes reveal the deep love and support of the Association for Free Will Baptist Family Ministries. They also reveal the importance of the Cumberland Association to the Children's Home ministry.

79th session 1922 - *D.B. Sassor, delegate from the General Conference of North Carolina made a talk on Educational and Orphanage work.*

96th session 1939 - Mrs. Fannie Polston was appointed as Chairman of the *Orphanage Committee.* Brother I.L. Stanley led the music for all sessions.

Brother I.L. Stanley is identified as the Superintendent of the Orphanage and reported the following: *The orphanage has 170 acres of land, good barn and fine water system. The Orphanage needs, Stock such as mules or horses, pigs and a cow that the children might have milk.*

100th session 1943 - *Brother Paul Woolsey reported that the Association had bought more than $1,100 in War Bonds for the Orphanage.*

103rd session 1946 – Orphanage
- *By recent action of the Board of Directors of the Tennessee Free Will Baptist Orphanage, the name of our home was changed to the Free Will Baptist Home for Children.*
- *There are 31 children at the home at this time.*
- *The crops have been good this year.*
- *A new barn has been erected at an expense of $504.16.*

130th session 1973 - *Reverend James Earl Raper gave the Children's Home report.*

144th session 1987 - *A.J. Looper from the Children's Home was recognized.*

150th session 1993 – *Roger Hood, Director of the Tennessee Children's Home, gave a report of the work.*

152nd session 1995 – *Jack Taylor brought greetings from Free Will Baptist Family Ministries.*

154th session 1997 - *Dr. James Kilgore, Director of Free Will Baptist Family Ministries, brought greetings.*

163rd session 2006 – *Brother Bob Shockey gave the Free Will Baptist Family Ministries report.*

165th session 2008 - *Brother Larry Hampton gave the Free Will Baptist Family Ministries report.*

166th session 2009 - *Brother Tim York gave the Free Will Baptist Family Ministries Report. He asked the body to remember Larry and Yvonne Hampton in our prayers. He also asked for us to remember Brother James Kilgore, the Director of the Family Ministries, as he battles cancer.*

167th session 2010 - *Brother Glenn Poston gave the Free Will Baptist Family Ministries report in brother Larry Hampton's absence.*

169th session 2012 – *Brother Mike Bell spoke for Free Will Baptist Family Ministries. He informed the group that the ministry has had several changes in leadership. The new director is brother Frank Wood.*

170th session 2013 - *Brother Mike Bell spoke for Free Will Baptist Family Ministries.*

171st session 2014 - *Brother Mike Bell spoke for Free Will Baptist Family Ministries. Bell thanked the churches for allowing him to come and share the ministry of the Family Ministries. The Family Ministries is celebrating 75 years of ministry today.*

173rd session 2016 - *Brother Eddie Hodges spoke for Free Will Baptist Family Ministries. Hodges presented pictures of some of the work.*

174th session 2017 - Brother Eddie Hodges spoke for Free Will Baptist Family Ministries. Over $30,000 has come in to the ministry from the association. He reviewed the various ways you can be involved in helping with funds.

Free Will Baptist Family Ministries

The Cumberland Association has been a vital part of the success of Free Will Baptist Family Ministries. What began as a burden from a group of Christian women of the Tennessee FWB Women's Auxiliary to find a place where our denomination could care for hurting children, subsequently birthed the FWB Home for Children in 1938.

Much of the success is a direct product of the prayers and support that have come from our wonderful friends of the Cumberland Association. Many of those who sacrificially gave of their time and efforts have already gone on to be with the Lord, but what a reunion of those that will be in Heaven as a result of the desire of His faithful servants to see a place that cared for orphan children.

Because of your continued friendship, now going on almost 80 years, God has allowed us to reach out and provide services encompassing the entire scope of the family, from the precious unborn to our saintly seniors.

I mean this statement with all my heart; "We could not do what we do without our supporters, and we are grateful to call the Cumberland Association our dear friends".

Many thanks and appreciation for your loyal service in His Kingdom work here on Earth.

Reverend Frank Woods, *Executive Director*

174th Cumberland Association Meeting Minutes

Selected sections were copied directly from the 2017 minutes. Individual contact information was removed.

By

Roy W. Harris

The 174th Session of the Cumberland Association of Free Will Baptists
October 21, 2017
First Free Will Baptist Church
1701 Hwy 96 South, Dickson, TN 37029
Reverend Eddie Thomas, Pastor

8:30 A.M. - Registration
9:00 A.M. – Session Opens
    Song – "We Will Glorify the King of Kings"
    Welcome - Reverend Eddie Thomas, Pastor
    Response, Scripture Reading, and Prayer - Reverend Dwayne James

9:15 A.M. – 174th Session of the Cumberland Association of Free Will Baptists officially called to order - Moderator Dr. Roy Harris introduced.

1. Seating of Delegate
2. Executive Board Report – Patrick Layton
3. Clerk's Report – Patrick Layton

4. Treasurer's Report – Patrick Layton
5. Christian Education Board Report – Phillip Morgan
6. Ministerial Benevolence Board Report – Reverend Jon Justice
7. International Missions Board Report
8. Cumberland Youth Camp Board Report – Reverend Stan Coker
9. Cumberland District WAC Report – Mrs. Judy Lytle
10. Local Quarterly Association Reports
 Northern Quarterly Report – Reverend Dwayne James
 South Central Quarterly Report – Reverend Mark Elliot
 Southern Quarterly Report – Reverend David Weeks
 Western Quarterly Report – Reverend Carl Hooper
11. State Ministries
 TN Promotional Office – Reverend Glenn Poston
 Election of Delegates for the Tennessee State Meeting (Nov. 13-15)
 Free Will Baptist Family Ministries – Reverend Eddie Hodges
12. Break 10:30 - 10:45 A.M.
13. Greetings and Misc. Reports
14. Registration Committee Report
15. Resolutions Committee Report
16. Obituary Committee Report
17. Old Business
18. New Business
19. Final report of the Nominating Committee
 Adjourn to Worship Service
11:30 A.M. Worship Service – Dr. Matthew J. Pinson, Welch College President

12:30 P.M. - Lunch (The Presbytery will meet during the lunch hour.)

ANNOUNCEMENTS

Next year's 175th session will be hosted by the Southern Quarterly on October 20, 2018 at Welch College, 1045 Bison Trail, Gallatin, TN. 37066.

DIRECTORY OF THE CUMBERLAND ASSOCIATION OFFICERS

Moderator: Reverend Roy Harris

Assistant Moderator: Reverend Jon Justice

Clerk/Treasurer: Patrick Layton

Assistant Clerk: Megan Morgan

Northern Quarterly Moderator: Reverend Dwayne James

Southern Quarterly Moderator: Reverend David Weeks

South Central Quarterly Moderator: Reverend Mark Elliott

Western Quarterly Moderator: Reverend Carl Hooper

BOARDS OF THE CUMBERLAND ASSOCIATION

INTERNATIONAL MISSIONS

MINISTERIAL BENEVOLENCE

Ronnie Smith	(2018)	Ray Lewis	(2018)
Ed Gragg	(2019)	Ed Gragg	(2019)
Ronald Mashburn	(2020)	Steve Phillips	(2020)

Russell Houske   (2021)   Bud Hill   (2021)
Craig Batts   (2022)

CHRISTIAN EDUCATION
Jeff Edgmon (2018)   Jeff Nichols   (2018)
Chris Talbot (2019)   Frank Owens   (2019)
Mike Keel   (2019)   Chad Kivette   (2020)
Josh Clark   (2020)

YOUTH CAMP

2018 David Brown   Stanley Cochran   Russell Houske
2019 Sam Johnson   Corey Minter
      Carol Reid   Len Scott
2020 Patrick Layton   Margaret Hampton
      Steve Greenwood   Tommy Dubois

TREASURERS TO WHOM FUNDS ARE SENT

Family Ministries: Reverend Frank Woods
International Missions: Mr. Adam Clagg
Welch College: Mr. Craig Mahler
National Association Of Free Will Baptists
State Home Missions: **Send to Tennessee State Association and designate to Tennessee Home Missions.**

Cumberland Youth Camp   Reverend Stan Coker
Tennessee State Association   Reverend Ray Lewis
Ministerial Benevolence   Reverend Jon Justice
Cumberland Association: Patrick Layton

CUMBERLAND ASSOCIATION UNIFIED GIVING PLAN
It is suggested that each church within the Cumberland give 10% of their undesignated offerings to their Quarterly

or to the Cumberland Association for the support of the Cumberland programs. The giving is as follows:

Don and Billie Sexton Memorial Missions Gift	10%
Tennessee Home Missions Board	10%
Welch College	10%
Cumberland Association	10%
Cumberland Ministerial Benevolence	15%
TN State Association	15%
Cumberland Youth Camp	30%
TOTAL	100%

PROCEEDINGS

MORNING SESSION–9:00 A.M.

The Cumberland Association met at the First Free Will Baptist Church in Dickson, TN on October 21, 2017. Brother Eddie Thomas led the gathering in singing "We Will Glorify the King of Kings". Brother Eddie Thomas welcomed the congregation and pointed out the location of the bathrooms. Brother Dwayne James thanked the host church and read from Philippians 1:1-6. He then led the body in prayer.

MORNING BUSINESS – 9:15 A.M.

The 174th meeting of the Cumberland Association was called to order by Patrick Layton, Clerk. Dr. Roy Harris, Moderator, thanked the body for coming and the First Free Will Baptist Church of Dickson and the Western Quarterly for hosting the meeting. All the ministers, deacons, and delegates were seated. Harris thanked the Nominating Committee for their work. Harris reviewed the committees of the Cumberland Association and the members of those committees. Harris reviewed the Rules of Decorum.

The executive board report was read and approved. The Clerk's Report for the 2015-2016 year was reviewed and approved.

Layton gave the Treasurer's Report and presented the Proposed Budget for 2016-2017. A motion and second were made to adopt the report and proposed budget. Harris explained the ideas and process of the formation of the committee, the writing of a book for the 175th Celebration of the Cumberland Association, and the location of the meeting. The motion carried.

Brother Phillip Morgan gave the Cumberland Christian Education Board Report and presented a proposed budget. There was a motion and second to receive the report and adopt the proposed budget; the motion carried. A partial Nominating Committee report was given for the Christian Education Board. A motion and second was made to approve the nominations.

Jon Justice gave the Ministerial Benevolence Board Report. He gave the Financial Report for 2016-2017. We currently have no recipients of the fund. There was a motion and a second to accept the report; the motion carried. A partial Nominating Committee report was given for the Ministerial Benevolence Board. A motion and second were made to approve the nomination and the motion carried. Justice presented the new idea for the ministerial benevolence board. There was a motion and second to adopt the new plan for the Ministerial Benevolence Board. Questions were asked and answered concerning the plan. The motion carried.

There was no report given by the Tennessee International Missions Board. A partial Nominating Committee report was given for the Tennessee International Missions Board. A motion and second were made to approve the nominations and the motion carried.

Brother Stan Coker, Camp Director, gave the Cumberland Youth Camp Report. Sometimes we hear the word "No". This summer we had to say "no" to some kids (approximately 25 kids). Coker thanked the association for their support. The Hayes Conference Center has allowed us to expand our ministry opportunity. This summer the camp ministered to 576 campers plus 36 day campers. The camp board has approved a plan for the addition of "flex" housing. The "flex" housing will serve for adult housing, camper housing, family housing, minister housing. Codes has approved the go ahead and the Water Department has approved to put four of these on one septic tank. Coker hopes to have plans from the architect by the beginning of the week. The camp is asking for donations for the housing needs. Coker wants to be a good steward of God's resources. He also presented the proposed budget for 2018. A motion and second was made to accept the report and adopt the proposed budget as given; the motion was approved. A partial Nominating Committee report was given for the Cumberland Youth Camp. There was a motion and second to approve the nominations; the motion carried.

There was no report given by the Cumberland Women Nationally Active for Christ.

Moderator Dwayne James gave the report of the Northern Quarterly. There was no report given by the South Central Quarterly. Moderator David Weeks gave the report of the Southern Quarterly. Moderator Carl Hooper gave the report of the Western Quarterly. The reports were received and approved as information. Harris thanked the moderators for their hard work throughout the year.

Brother Glenn Poston presented the Tennessee

Promotional Director's Report. He reported on the continued work of Tennessee Free Will Baptist in our denomination.

A motion was made and second to approve Pam Kennedy and Steve Pate as delegates and give the Moderator approval to appoint the other three delegates at the State meeting. The motion carried.

Brother Earl Langley brought a report to the association concerning the work of the Manchester church. The Carmack's have relocated to the area and a lot of work has been put into the church. The church has purchased an old furniture store next to the church to use as a new auditorium. Carmack sent out a letter requesting funds/materials for the remodeling of the building. Langley encouraged our churches to get involved in helping with this work.

Brother Eddie Hodges spoke for Free Will Baptist Family Ministries. Over $30,000 has come in to the ministry from the association. He reviewed the various ways you can be involved in helping with funds. The "Hands To Help" helps seniors in their homes. On December 1, the "Door of Hope" opened and is an extension of the Hope Center. On July 28, there was a ribbon cutting on the "Young's Children's Home". A new assisted living program has opened in Limestone, TN. He encouraged us to pray for and continue to financially support all those that serve and those that are being ministered too.

Brother Clayton Hampton presented his mission work in Montana. He has started his itinerary. He asked to be allowed to present at our churches. Please keep this work in your prayers.

Brother Chad Kivette presented the mission work at 180 Free Will Baptist Church. There was a man saved last

Sunday. The church will be going self-supporting at the end of the year. The church is hosting a men's retreat on September 13-15 at Cumberland Camp. David Crowe, Shiloh Hackett, Jim McComas, and Tom Malone will be speaking. During the day on Friday, there will be activities. A flyer was made available on the retreat.

      Harris called for the reports of the committees. Brother Cecil Boswell gave the Registration and Finance report. A motion and second was made to receive the report. The motion carried. Brother Billy Ellis brought the Resolutions Report. There were two resolutions. The first resolution was "Whereas every person on earth has descended from one family created in God's image, and whereas, we are called to go into all the world to carry the Gospel, and whereas, the Kingdom of God is, and will be made up of every tribe, kindred, tongue, and nation, and whereas, recent instigations and reactions in our state and in our country have brought about divisions along racial and ethnic lines, be it resolved that the Cumberland Association of Free Will Baptist reaffirm our commitment to efforts to reach, minister to, and be in full fellowship with all, without regard to racial or ethnic divisions, and that we promote an attitude of this fellowship in our individual churches." A motion and second were made to approve the resolution. Brother Roy Jensen made a motion to amend the motion to include a news release to appropriate outlets. The motion was seconded and the amendment carried. The motion carried. The second resolution was "Whereas, First Free Will Baptist Church Dickson has opened its doors to us with hospitality, and has welcomed us and prepared for us, be it resolved that we give them a rising vote of appreciation and thanks for this hospitality." A motion and second were made to approve the resolution.

The motion carried. Brother Jon Murray gave the Obituary Report. A prayer was offered by Brother Jon Murray for the families of those that had passed away. The motion to receive the report with great appreciation was seconded and approved.

There was one item of "New Business." There was a motion and second to give today's offering to the 175th Celebration of the Cumberland Association Fund. The motion carried.

Harris gave the final Nominating Committee report. The officers were taken one at a time. There was a motion and second to approve each officer for 2018 and the motions carried.

Harris thanked the body for their cooperation and helping move the meeting smoothly. Harris adjourned the business meeting.

MORNING WORSHIP-11:30 A. M.

Brother Eddie Thomas led the congregation in singing "Majesty." Brother Eddie Thomas called for the offering and prayed over it. Special music was provided by the host church. Brother Phillip Morgan introduced Dr. Matthew J. Pinson, Welch College President, as the worship speaker.

Pinson thanked the Executive Board for the opportunity to speak. Pinson brought his discussion on "The Reformation at 500: Why It Matters For Us Today." Pinson closed the message in prayer.

Brother Eddie Thomas shared directions for the meal. The Presbytery will meet during the lunch hour.

A motion and second was made to adjourn. The meeting was closed in prayer by Brother Aaron Harris.

Cumberland Executive Board Report
October 21, 2017

The Cumberland Executive Board Meeting met on April 18, 2016 at Welch College. The members present for the April meeting were Roy Harris (Moderator), Patrick Layton (Clerk/Treasurer), Mark Elliott (SCQ), Jon Justice (Assistant Moderator), Philip Morgan (Proxy for the Assistant Clerk/CE Board Chairman), and Dwayne James (NQ). The agenda for the meeting was adopted. The August meeting was changed from August 15th to August 8th. The meeting would take place at the Five Points Free Will Baptist Church.

The minutes of the last Executive Board Meeting were reviewed by Layton; the minutes were approved. Layton presented and reviewed a Bank Reconciliation Summary of Deposits and Disbursements and Annual Financial Report for 2016-2017 to date (See full report for details); the report was approved.

Harris mentioned that the Cumberland Association Meeting in 2018 will be the 175th meeting of the association. It will be hosted by the Southern Quarterly.

Harris entertained ideas for the theme of the Cumberland Association Meeting. Morgan mentioned that this year would be the 500th anniversary of the Reformation. A motion and second was made to pursue a theme based on the idea of the impact of the Reformation on today's church; the motion carried. A motion and second was made to ask Dr. Pinson to be the speaker; the motion carried.

The item of "Old Business" concerned the future of the Ministerial Benevolence Board. The board is requesting that the committee meet and come up with some ideas before the August meeting. There were no items of "New

Business".

The 2017 Cumberland Association meeting will take place on October 21, 2017 at the First Free Will Baptist Church in Dickson, Tennessee. The meeting will be hosted by the Western Quarterly.

The next Executive Board meeting will take place on Tuesday, August 8. Harris expressed his thanks for the work of the committee. Items of prayer were mentioned. The meeting was closed in prayer.

The Cumberland Executive Board Meeting was held on August 8, 2017 at Five Points Free Will Baptist. The members present for the August meeting were Roy Harris (Moderator), Patrick Layton (Clerk/Treasurer), Mark Elliott (SCQ), Jon Justice (Assistant Moderator), Tim McDonald (WQ), David Weeks (SQ), Stan Coker (Cumberland Camp Director). McDonald brought a devotion from Matthew 24:24 and opened the meeting in prayer. The agenda for the meeting was adopted.

Coker brought the report from Cumberland Camp. The camp is in the best financial shape it has ever been in. The camp currently has $106,000 in the bank. The camp received a grant for $32,000 from the Foundation for housing. Pray for wisdom concerning housing. The camp had 576 campers this summer. An eighteen-hole disc golf has been put in which was paid for by donations. Paintball was replaced with laser tag. There was a motion and second to receive the report; the motion carried. McDonald expressed thankfulness for Coker. Questions were asked and answered. Harris thanked Coker for the impact that he and the camp have made on his family and grandchildren.

The minutes of the last Executive Board Meeting were reviewed by Layton. There was a motion and second to approve the minutes; the motion carried. Layton presented and reviewed a Bank Reconciliation Summary of Deposits and Disbursements and Annual Financial Report for 2016-2017 to date. (See full report for details) There was a motion and second to approve the financial report; the motion carried.

Justice met with the Ministerial Benevolence Board. Mrs. Hornberger is the only recipient of the fund. She has been moved to a nursing home and the money has been going to keep up her house, which her son is living in. The board will meet Thursday. A system like the one that Carolina uses has been suggested for Ministerial Benevolence funds. There was a motion second to receive the report; the motion carried.

Harris presented ideas concerning the 175th Cumberland Association Celebration. The meeting will be held at Welch College and the college will provide the meal. A motion and second was made to allow the moderator to appoint a five-person steering committee with the moderator to serve as the chairman; the motion carried. A motion and second was made to authorize Harris to pursue the publication of a book for the 175th Cumberland Association Celebration; the motion carried.

The proposed budget for 2017-2018 year was reviewed by the body. A line item was added for the Cumberland Association 175th Celebration. The proposed amount designated for the celebration was $1000. The other totals for the budget were left the same. A motion and second was made to recommend the proposed budget to the Association.

Harris reviewed the theme, speaker, and location of the annual meeting. Lunch will be provided and the Presbytery will meet during the lunch.

The next Executive Board meetings will take place on

April 17, 2018 and August 7, 2018. Harris expressed his thanks to Weeks for hosting the meeting. Items of prayer were mentioned. The meeting was closed in prayer by Justice.
Respectfully Submitted,
Patrick Layton, Clerk

REPORT OF COMMITTEE ON COMMITTEES

Saturday, October 21, 2017
(* Denotes Committee Chairman)

REGISTRATION AND FINANCE

    Cecil Boswell*
    Eddie Hodges
    Clayton Hampton

NOMINATING

    Jason Bell*
    Judson Phenice
    Steve Phillips
    Mark Elliott

OBITUARY

    John Murray*
    Eddie Thomas
    Roy Jenson
    Steve Swango

RESOLUTIONS

    Billy Ellis*
    Rick Kennedy

Respectfully Submitted,
Clayton Hampton, Billy Ellis, Eric Puschman, Mark Elliott

QUARTERLY REPORTS

NORTHERN QUARTERLY REPORT

I bring you greetings from the 23 churches that

make up the Northern Quarterly. We had three Quarterly meetings this year, conducted business, enjoyed time around God's Word, and always have a great time of fellowship. We also continue to enjoy sweet fellowship among our pastors each Wednesday as we meet for coffee and conversation at the Wendy's in Pleasant View. We also enjoy our fellowship breakfast the first Tuesday of each month at the Shoney's in Springfield. Pleasant View Christian School is in its 40th year of operation and is continuing to grow and be a blessing to the community. The last Sunday in February every year, our Churches participate in Welch College Day where we are blessed to have faculty from the college speak at our churches that Sunday morning. On Sunday evening, we gather at Pleasant View Christian School for a rally. The purpose for the day is to raise funds for the Ketteman Student Scholarship Program. We praise the Lord for what he is doing among our churches.

Respectfully Submitted, Reverend Dwayne James (Northern Quarterly Moderator)

SOUTHERN QUARTERLY REPORT

Moderator David Weeks reported for the Southern Quarterly. The Quarterly has 16 churches. The meetings included the following speakers and topics: Brother Tommy Swindol – Reaching People, Brother Matthew Bracey – Sexuality/Gender. He is encouraging the Southern Quarterly to give $500 to help with the 175h Celebration of the Cumberland Association.

SOUTH CENTRAL QUARTERLY REPORT

The South Central Quarterly met twice this year.

Our January meeting was canceled due to bad weather and was not rescheduled. The April meeting was held at Loyal Chapel with Stan Coker from Cumberland Camp as the guest speaker. The July meeting was held at Berean with Ken Akers, Director of the Master's Men department as guest speaker.

WESTERN QUARTERLY REPORT

Moderator Carl Hooper gave the report. He brought greetings from the Western Quarterly. The Western Quarterly met four times during the past year. Our meetings are well attended both by our own estimation and the comments of our visitors. We continue to emphasize the fellowship and worship aspects of our meetings and our people respond positively. Our speakers included Dr. Eagleton, Brother Waynick, and Brother Street. The Quarterly pastors enjoy a time of fellowship once a month at the Plantation Restaurant in Dickson. We, of the Western Quarterly, look forward to serving our Lord with you in the year ahead.
In Christ, Carl Hooper (Western Quarterly Moderator)

MINISTERIAL BENEVOLENCE

Ministerial Benevolence Board Report
10/01/16 - 10/20/17

Balance Forward 10/01/16	$ 9,985.08
Reported Income 10/1/16 – 10/20/17	$ 3,288.88
Total accounted for	$13,273.96

Disbursements:
Mrs. Jean Hornberger $2,750.00

Board Exp. (Meal)	$	55.57
Clerk	$	200.00
Total Disbursed		$3,005.57
Total Accounted for:		$13,273.96
Total Disbursed		$ 3,005.57
Balance 8/8/2017		$10,268.39

GUIDELINES FOR MINISTERIAL BENEVOLENCE BOARD

1. **Membership**. Any ordained Free Will Baptist minister (or his wife) holding a card of good standing from the Cumberland Association of Free Will Baptist Presbytery may enroll. The purpose of this ministry is to provide needed money, as quickly as possible, to a spouse or other benefactor as designated by the member upon said member's death.
2. **Enrollment**. An enrollment fee of $10.00 per participant will be charged. Each minister (or his wife) will the pay a participation fee of $35.00. The church he pastors or attends may desire to pay these fees on behalf of the minister. In order to receive appropriate notification concerning deaths and contribution renewal it is important that you keep your information current with the Benevolent Fund Board.
3. The $35.00 fee will be placed in a special savings account for the purpose of drawing interest.
4. Upon the death of a participating member, the Benevolent Fund will pay $35.00 per member of the group to the surviving spouse or other benefactor

designated by the member.
5. Upon notice by the Benevolent Fund Board that a member has died, and payment mad, all other members are required to submit another payment of $35.00 to the Benevolent Fund within 30 days, or be dropped from the benevolent membership.
6. Any individual having enrolled in the Benevolent Fund may remain a member as long as they participate with their contributions even if they move outside the Cumberland Association.
7. There will be a thirty (30) day waiting period following the date of enrollment before membership is effective. If a death should occur within the first thirty (30) days, the enrollment fee and the members participation fee will be refunded to the spouse or other benefactor designated by the member.
8. The fund shall be administered by the Ministerial Benevolence Board of the Cumberland Association of Free Will Baptists.
9. Any changes, alterations, and or amendments shall be made upon approval of the Cumberland Association of Free Will Baptists.

TREASURER'S REPORT
CUMBERLAND ASSOCIATION OF FREE WILL BAPTISTS
10/01/16 - 9/30/17

Beginning Checking Account Balance $7,502.71
Receipts
Cumberland Association Dues   1,475.00
State Association Dues   8,850.00
National Association Dues   8,850.00
Other Gifts   586.59

Interest Income	176.52		
TN State Association UGMP	3,585.94		
Total Receipts	**$23,524.05**		

Distributions

TN State Association Dues	8,850.00		
National Association Dues	8,850.00		
Treasurers Fee	350.00		
Clerks Fee	350.00		
Cumberland Association CE Board	1,250.00		
180 Free Will Baptist Church (Offering)	498.00		
Bank Fees	0.00		
Web Site Maintenance	144.00		
Executive Board Expense	88.80		
TN State Association UGMP*			
Cumberland Camp		30%	1,075.78
State Office		15%	537.90
Ministerial Benevolence Board		15%	537.90
International Missions		10%	358.60
TN. Home Missions		10%	358.60
Welch College		10%	358.60
Total Distributions			**$23,608.18**
Ending Cash Balance			**$ 7,418.58**

*10% of UGDP stays in Cumberland Association

Respectfully submitted,

Patrick Layton, Treasurer

CUMBERLAND ASSOCIATION OF FREE WILL BAPTIST
PROPOSED BUDGET 10/01/17 – 9/30/18

Beginning Checking Account Balance   **$7,418.58**
Receipts

Cumberland Association Dues (60 churches x $25.00)
$ 1,500.00
State Association Dues   (60 churches x $150.00)
$ 9,000.00
National Association Dues   (60 churches x $150.00)
$ 9,000.00
Other Gifts $ 500.00
Interest Income $ 125.00
TN State Association UGMP (3% coming back to Cumberland) $ 3,200.00
Total Receipts   **$23,325.00**

Distributions

TN State Association Dues (60 churches x $150.00)
$ 9,000.00
National Association Dues (60 churches x $150.00)
$ 9,000.00
Treasurers Fee $ 350.00
Clerks Fee $ 350.00
Executive Board Expense $ 150.00
Cumberland Web Site Hosting $ 144.00
Cumberland Association CE Board $ 1,250.00
Bank Fees $ 10.00
Cumberland Association 175th Celebration $ 1,000.00
TN State Association UGMP
    Cumberland Camp   30% $ 1,000.00
    State Office   15% $ 500.00
    Ministerial Benevolence Board 15% $ 500.00
    Don and Billie Sexton Missions Memorial Gift.
                            10% $ 300.00
    TN Home Missions   10% $ 300.00
    Welch College   10% $ 300.00

Total Distributions
$24,154.00

Projected Ending Checking Account Balance
$ 6,589.58

FEARLESS
Cumberland Camp 2017

For God has not given us a spirit of fear, but of power and of love and of a sound mind. (2 Timothy 1:7)

- What would you do for Christ if you were not afraid?
- Is your life characterized by power, love, and self control?
- How would our lives be impacted if our fear was replaced with a courageous faith?

Campers this year were confronted by these powerful questions, and the Biblical truths behind them as they attended Cumberland Youth Camp. Another record number of attendees (576 residential, 36 day campers) enjoyed all that camp has to offer: activities, food, friends, all wrapped in a spiritual emphasis. Parents seemed to appreciate the added choice of two weeks for teens (one for high school and another for all teens) along with two weeks specifically for junior age and a combo week (junior and junior high age). Enrollment exceeded expectation and capacity (see chart below). To God be the glory.

Dates, Age Group, Director, Evangelist and # of Campers

Dates	Age Group	Director	Evangelist	# of Campers
May 28-Jn 2	High School	Corey Minter	Edwards, Puschmann	100
June 4-9	Teen	David Dell	Chris Davenport	107
June 11-16	Junior 1	Steve Greenwood	Josh Wooten	133
June 18-23	Junior 2	Brian Lewis	Jon Forrest	77
June 25-30	Combo	Craig Batts	Craig Batts	159

We continue to make improvements and additions to the camp ministry. Disc Golf is our newest offering, with an 18 hole course weaving a wooded path around the main campus area. We also shifted from paintball to laser tag, a change that was well received by our guests, with over 500 participating this summer alone.

Financial support for your camp continues strong. Every dollar that we receive could have gone somewhere else and represents the sacrificial generosity of God's people. We are so thankful for churches and individuals that share their blessings with us.

Housing for our campers is at a premium right now. Several special gifts, including a grant from the FWB Foundation, in the last year have prompted your board to consider what God would have us do. Please pray that we will know His will and pursue it.

Important Dates for 2018
Re3 (Pastor's Wife's Retreat) Jan 26-28
High School Camp (grades 9-12) May 27-June1
Teen (Ages 12-18) June 3-8
Junior 1 (Ages 7-11) June 10-15
Junior 2 (Ages 7-11) June 17-22
Combo (Ages 7-14) June 24-29
We love serving the Lord with you. Keep in touch.

Stan Coker
2193 Happy Hills Acres Rd.
Woodlawn, TN 37191
(931)647-5111

Cumberland Youth Camp
Proposed 2018 Budget

Income
Contributions
    Surplus Sales $ 1,550.00
    General Offerings $ 66,950.00
    Friends of Camp $ 31,500.00
Total Contributions $ 100,000.00

Fee Income
    Paintball $ 11,500.00

Camp Registrations	$110,000.00
Retreat Registration	$ 2,500.00
Rental Income	$ 76,000.00
Total Fee Income	$200,000.00

Operations		
Canteen Income	$ 8,240.00	
Miscellaneous	$ 100.00	
Total Operations Income		$ 8,340.00

Grand Total Income	$308,340.00

Expenses

Building and Grounds		$ 80,000.00
Office Expense		$ 20,000.00
Salary and Benefits		
Director	$ 63,685.00	
Camp Manager	$ 15,285.00	
Maintenance manager	$ 780.00	
Yard Care	$ 4,000.00	
Christmas Bonus	$ 750.00	
Total Salary and Benefits		$ 84,500.00

Mileage	$ 9,800.00
Camp Expenses	$ 75,000.00
Retreat Expenses	$ 2,500.00
Rental Expenses	$ 25,000.00
Canteen Expenses	$ 7,500.00
Grand Total Expenses	$ 304,300.00

Net Income	$ 4,040.00

The Cumberland Association of Free Will Baptist Christian Education Board Report to the Cumberland Association Executive Committee of Free Will Baptists
October 21, 2017

For the past few years, our board has primarily worked to financially support pre-existing Christian education events in our association. Several of our churches had been offering Sunday school training, short conferences, and the like. However, none of the events we normally support were provided this year. As a result, we did not carry out any major event this year. However, we have begun discussing sending financial support to the Free Will Baptist church and school in St. Croix, U.S. Virgin Islands that has been affected by the recent hurricanes. We are also exploring the possibility of holding a luncheon for pastors with Dr. Robert Picirilli serving as our speaker.

Respectfully submitted,
Phillip T. Morgan, Chairman

Promotional Director's Report
Cumberland Association
October 21, 2017

The state office has been blessed with another good year. There are a lot of good things going on throughout the state. Our churches are engaging the culture and working hard to reach their communities for Christ. Our pastors seem to be more determined to bloom where God has planted them and it appears that the length of tenure is being extended.

Financially, the support of our various ministries is strong. While undesignated giving is down slightly this year, designated giving through the state office is up an impressive 22 percent. Total income through the state treasurer is up over 16 percent. We give glory and praise to God that our treasurer accounted for over one million dollars this year. This is the first year this has happened except for the year the endowment was given in 2012 and is the best year in our history.

We are happy to report that our state boards have had adequate funding. Please keep in mind that our state boards as well as the state office operates primarily on "undesignated funds." While we rejoice that our churches feel the burden to designate the bulk of their gifts to various ministries like International Missions, North American Ministries, Welch College and Family Ministries, please don't forget that undesignated gifts through the Unified Ministry Plan provide the means for scholarships to Welch College, expenses for board members to attend meetings, funding for the promotional director to operate in a full-time capacity, printing of the digest, minutes, and other miscellaneous expenses.

All nine of our associations are engaged to some extent in the state work. I have had the privilege to visit all of our associations on a regular basis and there has been great fellowship, unity, and camaraderie in all parts of the state. I am particularly thankful for the Cumberland Association and its generous support of the state work.

Our mission works have been doing well and both the Clarksville work and the Oakland work will go self-supporting at the end of the year. Family Ministries continues to grow and recently opened the John Reed assisted living and skilled nursing facility in Limestone, Tennessee. It is a beautiful facility on top of a hill overlooking the beautiful mountains in the area. Pray for Executive Director Frank Woods and his dedicated staff as they serve this thriving ministry.

  God is still calling men and women into His service and there is a greater interest in our preachers wanting to receive advanced training. While this is a time consuming process, in the long run, our men will be better equipped to handle the challenges of a changing world. There is a renewed excitement on the campus of Welch College since moving into the new campus. This excitement is seen in the eyes of the students as well as their parents. Many of our pastors are receiving training in other places. Online learning is by far the fastest growing area of ministerial training for most of our pastors in the state. This enables them to receive quality training without uprooting their families and leaving their ministries.

  Many of our young people are still answering the call to the regions beyond the borders of our own country. Our own International Missions Department has been developing partnerships with other mission agencies. Our state IM Board is actively engaged in challenging our churches to "Go Global." This is an exciting time for the church to be involved in global evangelism. Our young people are applying in great numbers for spots on our E-TEAM program and other opportunities to get involved in reaching the world. Almost $350,000 was given to IM through the state office this year compared to $271,000 last year.

  In conclusion, let me say, I consider it a high honor to serve Tennessee Free Will Baptists as promotional director. With God being my helper, I will to the best of my

ability promote the work of our boards, promote unity among our people, and promote the ministry of all our local churches as we labor together for our Lord, Jesus Christ. I would love to come to all of your churches to share about the ministry of the state office.
Humbly Yours,
Glenn Poston
Tennessee Promotional Director

Cumberland Association of Free Will Baptists Obituary Report October 1, 2016 – September 30, 2017

Northern Quarterly

Rex Collins	Bethel
Glenn Spain	Bethel
Steve Walker	Bethel
Jay Davis	Bethlehem
Mary Jane Watts	Bethlehem
Juanita Davenport	First Springfield
June Jones	First Springfield
Paula Herrnel	First Springfield
Bennie Schutte	First Springfield
Frances Lovie Allen	Friendship
Willie Estelle Chandler	Friendship
Malcolm Wayne Green	Friendship
Fannie Marie Knight	Friendship
Edith Moore	Good Springs
Bernice Nichols	Good Springs
Janice Faye Balthrop Douglas	Harper Road
Frances Ellis	Heads
Larry White	Heads
Steve Coots	Lakeview

Kenneth Dodson	Lakeview
Charles Balthrop	Oaklawn
Medena Forbes	Oaklawn
Travis Knox	Oaklawn
Marcia Jean Morris	Oaklawn
Frances Albright	Shady Grove
Carol Poole	Shady Grove
Ted Henry	Unity

South Central Quarterly

Ned Anderson	Berean
Geneva Pack	Berean
Nelda Fox	Berean
Ruth Hill	Faith
Joel Carlton Doss	Flatwoods
Joyce Marie Grisham	Flatwoods
Jonas Whitwell	Loyal Chapel

Southern Quarterly

Marshall Rumfelt	Cane Ridge
Frances Spencer	Cane Ridge
Maxine Wagner	Cane Ridge
Ruby Hunter	Cofer's Chapel
Geneva Walker	Corner Stone
Randy Bowman	Donelson Fellowship
C.A. Dobbs	Donelson Fellowship
Juanita Hingst	Donelson Fellowship
Bryant Raburn	Donelson Fellowship
Carl Sanders	Donelson Fellowship
Pearl Wilson	Donelson Fellowship
Dan Barnett	Five Points
Robert (Bob) Micheals	Madison
Charles Denson	Madison
Duncan Evans	Richland

Western Quarterly

Francis Smith	Carlisle
Thelma Delashmitt	Carlisle
Geneva Burgess Lankford	First FWB Dickson
Billy Albright	First FWB Dickson
Bill Kizer	First FWB Waverly
Carolyn Groffis	First FWB Waverly
Gail Lyell	Miller's Chapel
Cecil Earhart	Pleasant Hill
Lori Lane	Pleasant Hill
JoAnn Tummins	Unite

REGISTRATION AND FINANCE REPORT

Ministers: 46, Delegates: 18, Deacons: 3
Visitors: 25   TOTAL = 92

The offering received was $280.00.

RESOLUTION COMMITTEE REPORT

The Resolution Committee submits the following recommendations:

1. Whereas every person on earth has descended from one family created in God's image, and whereas, we are called to go into all the world to carry the Gospel, and whereas, the Kingdom of God is, and will be made up of every tribe, kindred, tongue and nation, and whereas, recent instigations and reactions have brought about divisions along racial and ethnic lines in our state and in our country, be it resolved that the Cumberland Association reaffirm our commitment to efforts to reach, minister to, and be in full fellowship with all, without regard to racial or ethnic divisions, and that we promote an attitude of this fellowship in our individual churches.

Whereas, First Free Will Baptist Church Dickson has opened its doors to us with hospitality, and as welcomed us and prepared for us, Be it resolved that we give them a rising vote of appreciation and thanks for this hospitality.

NOMINATING COMMITTEE REPORT

We, the nominating committee, submit the following report.

Cumberland Camp Board:
Tommy Dubose replacing Tommy Dubose (2020)
Steve Greenwood replacing Steve Greenwood (2020)
Margaret Hampton replacing Margaret Hampton (2020)
Patrick Layton replacing Patrick Layton (2020)

Christian Education Board:
Jeff Edgmon filling the unexpired term of Max Perry (2018)
Chad Kivette replacing Chad Kivette (2020)
Josh Clark replacing Philip Morgan (2020)

Ministerial Benevolence Board:
Ray Lewis filling the unexpired term of Ed Fox (2018)
Craig Batts replacing Ronnie Smith (2022)

International Missions Board:
Russell Houske replacing Russell Houske (2021)

Officers
Roy Harris replacing Roy Harris (**Moderator**) (2019)
Jon Justice replacing Jon Justice (**Assistant Moderator**) (2019)
Patrick Layton replacing Patrick Layton (**Clerk/Treasurer**) (2019)
Megan Morgan replacing Megan Morgan (**Assistant Clerk**) (2019)

If any delegate has a name to place in nomination please do so.

Respectfully Submitted,

Clayton Hampton, Billy Ellis, Eric Puschman, and Mark Elliot

"The Reformation at 500: Why It Matters for Us Today"

Presented by Matthew Pinson

This month is the 500th anniversary of the Protestant Reformation. On October 31, 1517, Martin Luther nailed his Ninety-Five Theses to the door of the Castle Church in Wittenberg, Germany, to critique abuses in the late medieval Catholic Church.

The Reformation's relevance – "renewal through retrieval."

"Back to the sources" – "back to the fountains"
The Five Solas:
Sola Scriptura (scripture alone), *solus Christus* (Christ alone), *sola gratia* (grace alone), *sola fide* (faith alone), and *soli Deo gloria* (to God alone be the glory).

How Free Will Baptists Fit into the Protestant Reformation

America's first Free Will Baptists were English General Baptists who moved to this side of the Atlantic in the 1600s.

The English General Baptist River was made up of Anabaptist, Puritan, and Arminian streams that flowed into it. Each of these three movements came out of the Reformed movement associated with Zwingli and Calvin.

Our founder Thomas Helwys was an Arminianized radical Puritan who had rejected infant baptism.

Sola Gratia and Sola Fide: **Salvation by Grace Alone through Faith Alone**

Thomas Grantham: "That God imputes Righteousness to Men without Works, is so plain, that it can never be denied. What is thus imputed, is not acted by us, but expressly reckoned as a matter of free Gift, or Grace; and this can be the Righteousness of none but Christ . . . because no other way can the Righteousness of God be made ours . . . there is none righteous, no not one. Except therefore the Righteousness of Christ be laid hold on, there is no Righteousness to be imputed to Sinners." The relevance of sola gratia and sola fide for our doctrine of perseverance.

Solus Christus: **Christ Our Only Mediator**

The Reformation emphasis on salvation by Christ alone also meant that Christ was the only mediator between God and man (1 Tim. 2:5), our only priest.

Arminius said that, since Christ is "Mediator and the Head of his church, so that the church can pay this honor to NO ONE except him, without incurring the crime of idolatry; therefore, the papists, who adore Mary, the angels, or holy men, and who invoke them . . . as intercessors through their own merits, are guilty of the crime of idolatry." This teaching resulted in the doctrine of the priesthood of all believers.

William Jeffrey (1650s), writing against the authoritarianism of the Episcopalians and Presbyterians of his day: "The Lord Christ saith, that they which are accounted to rule over the Gentiles, exercise Lordship over them; and their great ones exercise authority upon them, but it shall not be so among you, *but whosoever will be great among you, shall be your servant, and whosoever will be chief of you, shall be servant of all,* Mark 10. 42-44. And therefore the

Elders who are the chief servants, are not to exercise Lordship over their Brethren, therefore not to rule without the Body, the Church. . . . so indeed it hath been, and is where the *Pope*, and Lord Bishops, and Presbytery hath the power, they make the members of their National, Generational way, *slaves* to serve with great burdens, and many of them are very ignorant."

Soli Deo Gloria: Glorifying God alone in Worship and in Life

Luther's "theology of the cross" vs. medieval Roman Catholicism's "theology of glory."

The Reformers wanted to rid worship of anything that could be construed as detracting in the least from God receiving all the glory. They also emphasized that all of live is lived to the glory of God.

Sola Scriptura: The Bedrock Foundation of the Reformation That Can Renew and Revitalize the Modern Church

Without Sola Scriptura, scripture alone, we never would have had any of the other solas, and there never would have been a Reformation.

Arminius said, "No subject can be mentioned, by the sole knowledge or the worship of which the church ought to bedeck herself with increased honour and dignity . . . which . . . is not comprehended in the Holy Scriptures. . . ."

Arminius: "The Papists indeed speak and write many things about Mary, the rest of the saints, and about the Roman Pontiff [or pope]; but we affirm that these are not objects either of any knowledge or worship which the church ought to bestow on them."

The Free Will Baptist Treatise says that the Scriptures

are "the only sufficient and infallible rule and guide to salvation and all Christian worship and service."

Grantham said: "Who can imagine that anything devised by men (though never so specious) can add any advantage to the way and worship of God; and if not, to what end are such additions made? And who seeth not, to add one ceremony, is the same as to add one thousand; if therefore we desire God's worship to be kept in purity; let all that love Christ beware of superstition altogether."

Sola Scriptura is *not* saying that we don't care about tradition, that we ignore 2,000 years of the Spirit's witness in the saints and martyrs of the Christian past. *Not* "no creed but the Bible."

How does the doctrine of sola scriptura apply to us today?

Temptation to be influenced by the secular thought in our theology

Temptation to be influenced by secular entertainment and marketing and big business and pop psychology in our church practice

We need to go back and drink deeply from the Reformation well of Sola Scripture. When we do this, it will change us deeply. It will renew and revitalize us. We'll realize anew and afresh that the Word of God is sufficient. We'll realize that God knows our needs better than we do, and that he has provided us in his word ALL we need to serve Him and share our faith and teach people his truth and live out our lives in the church.

Three areas of contrast between the Reformed and Catholics: Preaching, singing, leading

QUARTERLY CLERKS

Northern	South Central	Southern	Western
Megan Morgan	Kathy Brown	Anthony Poff	Debbie Elliott

NORTHERN QUARTERLY

Moderator Clerk
Dwayne James Megan Morgan

CHURCH	PASTOR	CLERK
Ashland City FWB	Reverend Wayne Bess, Jr.	Edith Perry
Bethel FWB Thornton	Reverend Barry Raper	Mrs. Pamela K.
Bethlehem FWB	Reverend Shiloh Hacket	Mrs. Ann Hyde
Covenant FWB	Dr. Danny Dwyer	Mrs. Judy Ray
First FWB Scott	Reverend Judson Phenice	Mrs. Mary Ann
Friendship FWB Hampton	Reverend Cecil Boswell	Mrs. Pamela B.
Good Springs FWB Whitworth	Reverend Randall Riggs	Mrs. Lori
Harper Road FWB	Reverend Gene Parton	Ms. Debbie Smith
Heads FWB	Reverend Billy Ellis	Mrs. Linda Morgan
Hendersonville FWB Sanschargrin	Reverend Reid Wilerson	Mrs. Ruby
Immanuel FWB	Reverend Jesse Owen	Mrs. Terri Cockrell
Lakeview Fellowship	Reverend Scott Bee	Ms. Cyndi Talley
Liberty FWB	Reverend Mike Callis	Mrs. Trina Osborne
Mt. Zion FWB	Vacant	Mrs. Connie Anderson
New Hope FWB	Reverend Corey Minte	Mrs. JoAnna Caira
Oakland FWB	Reverend Kenneth Clement	Ms. Diane Lyle
Oaklawn FWB	Reverend Brandon Bel	Mr. Marian P. Hunter
Oakwood FWB Minnehan	Reverend Dwayne James	Mrs. Betsy
Olivet FWB	Reverend Chris Camp	Mr. Daniel T.

McGregor		
Pardue Memorial FWB	Reverend Jason Bel	Ms. Sherry Bagwell
Shady Grove FWB	Dr. Ken Riggs	Mrs. Peggy Roberts
Unity FWB	Reverend Billy Bower	Ms. Marie Wright
West End FWB	Reverend Ronnie Smith	Mrs. Teresa Lewis

SOUTHERN QUARTERLY

Moderator		Clerk
Reverend David Weeks		Anthony Poff

CHURCH	PASTOR	CLERK
Cane Ridge FWB	Reverend Jason Willaford	Reverend Eugene Workman
Cofer's Chapel FWB	Reverend Allen Pointe	Mrs. Julie Steele
Corner Stone FWB	Reverend Aaron Harri	Ms. Betty Poff
Cross Timbers FWB	Reverend Craig Batt	Mrs. Temisia Brown
Donelson FWB	Reverend Tommy Swindol	Mrs. Debbie Warner
Five Points FWB	Reverend David Weeks	Mrs. Leigh Binkley
Franklin Community	Reverend Kevin Riggs	
LaVergne FWB	Reverend Steve Marcum	Mrs. Jean Welch
Madison FWB	Reverend John Murray	Mrs. Ruth Jackson
Manchester FWB	Reverend Charlie Carmack	Mr. Ronald Smitty
Rejoice FWB	Reverend Eric Puschmann	Mrs. Beverly Skiles
Richland FWB	Reverend Devon Jensen	Mrs. Joyce Worthington
Sylvan Park FWB	Reverend Frank Owens	Ms. LaDonna Owens
Trinity FWB	Reverend Vernon Martin	Mrs. Donna Walker
Truth and Grace	Reverend Richard Atwood	Mr. Marvin Briggs
Victory FWB	Reverend Thurman L. Page	

SOUTH CENTRAL QUARTERLY

Moderator	Clerk/Treasurer
Reverend Mark Elliott	Ms. Kathy Brown

CHURCH	PASTOR	CLERK
Berean FWB	Reverend Gary Lovitt	Ms. Mary Tidwell
Blue Springs FWB	Reverend Mark Elliott	Debbie Demastus
Crossroads FWB	Reverend Ronald Mashburn	Ms. Jessie Glass
Faith FWB	Reverend Billy Brown	Mrs. Polly Watson
Flatwoods FWB	Reverend Tom DuBose	Mrs. Peggy Peppers
Loyal Chapel FWB	Reverend Steve Swango	

WESTERN QUARTERLY

Moderator	Clerk
Reverend Carl Hooper	Patrick Layton

CHURCH	PASTOR	CLERK
Brandon's Chapel FWB	Reverend Josh Colson	Mrs. Lorienda Stafford
Carlisle FWB	Russell Houske	Mrs. Claire Taylor
Dunbar's Chapel FWB	Matthew Saunders	Mrs. Leahjon Heflin
First Dickson FWB	Reverend Eddie Thomas	Mrs. Clarissa Layton
First McEwen FWB	Reverend Tommy Street	Mrs. Anita Vineyard
First Waverly FWB	Reverend Rick Kennedy	Mrs. Sherry Forrester
Hurricane Chapel FWB	Reverend Tim Farris	Mrs. Mary Tummins
Millers Chapel FWB	Reverend James Black	Mrs. Gwen Minniehan
Oak Grove FWB	Reverend Tim McDonald	Mrs. Pam Wells
Pleasant Hill FWB	Reverend Steve Phillips	Mrs. Nelda

Saunders

Rock Springs FWB Reverend Matthew Honeycutt   Mrs. Amanda Tidwell

Scott's Chapel FWB   Reverend Artest Waynick   Mrs. Sharon Vanzant

Stoney Point FWB   Reverend Byron Bishop   Mrs. Evelyn Smith

United FWB   Vacant   Mrs. Lucy Dudley

Delegates to the Tennessee State Association

Mrs. Pam Kennedy

Mr. Josh Hampton
Mr. Bryce Darnell

The other two delegates will be appointed by the Moderator at the State Meeting

INTERNATIONAL MISSIONARIES FROM THE CUMBERLAND ASSOCIATION

Kenneth and Rejane Eagleton Family
Jerry and Barbara Gibbs Family
Heath and Joni Hubbard Family
Shannon Little
Donnie and Ruth McDonald Family
David and Angie Outlaw Family
Jonathan and Amy Postlewaite Family
Josh and Lydia Provow Family
Steve and Becky Riggs Family
Daniel and Katie Speer Family
Matthew and Brooke Turnbough Family

GOVERNMENT AND CONSTITUTION
CUMBERLAND ASSOCIATION OF FREE WILL BAPTISTS

ARTICLE 1. Each Quarterly holding membership in this District Association shall be entitled to five (5) delegates elected from the laity, with additional delegates from each member Church as follows: one delegate for the first 50 members or fraction thereof, and an additional delegate for each additional 50 members or fraction thereof. Furthermore, all ordained ministers and deacons holding membership in the Presbytery of this District Association shall be standing delegates.

ARTICLE 2. Each member Quarterly of this Association shall send a letter to each annual meeting giving information and statistics according to the form provided by the clerk of the association.

ARTICLE 3. This Association, when convened, shall be governed by Roberts Rules of Order.

ARTICLE 4. The Association shall elect a Moderator, Assistant Moderator, Clerk, Assistant Clerk, and Treasurer from its membership to serve two-year terms and may succeed themselves.

ARTICLE 5. New churches shall petition the Quarterly meeting for membership. The Quarterly shall have power to receive new churches as members, and in turn shall inform the District Association of their membership.

ARTICLE 6. The Association shall post minutes of each year's annual meeting on the Association's website in a form which may be downloaded and printed. A paper copy will also be kept in the archives of Free Will Baptist Bible College, Nashville, TN.

ARTICLE 7. Annual dues for each member Quarterly shall

consist of the current Quarterly dues plus the current Cumberland Association, Tennessee State Association, and National Association dues for each member church.

ARTICLE 8. For the purpose of ordaining ministers of the gospel and handling accusations of un-Christian conduct, there shall be a Presbytery, which shall convene at the close of the annual Association session. A meeting may be called at any time during the year by the Presbytery moderator and clerk or at the written request of five Presbytery members.

The Presbytery shall consist of ordained members present, and they shall elect a moderator, and clerk from among themselves who shall hold their offices until their successors are elected.

The membership of the Presbytery of the Cumberland Association shall consist of all ordained ministers and deacons holding cards of good standing in this Presbytery. Each quarterly meeting shall function as a subcommittee, and shall have the right to examine all applications for ordination or ratification of credentials, sent with recommendation from the churches composing the Quarterly Meeting, and if found competent, or ordain and set them apart for work by prayer and laying on of hands. The examining committee of each Quarterly Meeting shall make an annual report to the yearly meeting of the Cumberland Association Presbytery. Such report will also include the names of five elected members to serve as the examining committee of said Quarterly Meeting.

ARTICLE 9. It shall be the duty of each minister who shall organize a church to ordain deacons for the same. It is his duty, also, to ordain deacons where a vacancy occurs within his charge. It shall be the duty of each pastor to encourage the organization and support of the Sunday School in the church or churches where he is pastor as well as other organizations that may prove helpful to the work of the church.

ARTICLE 10. No persons shall be ordained to the ministry nor shall the credentials of any minister be ratified until he is qualified to meet the conditions stated in the third chapter of I Timothy. The term "the husband of one wife" means he shall not have more than one living wife (that is, he shall not be married to one wife at the present time and there be a wife still living from a previous marriage). This shall be tested by the Presbytery. The Presbytery shall have full power to propound such spiritual questions as they consider necessary to determine his qualifications. All candidates for ordination shall be required to answer these questions satisfactorily.

ARTICLE 11. Based on the teaching of Scripture, we believe that God creates each human being as either male or female. We also believe Scripture teaches that all human sexual relations are reserved exclusively within the bonds of marriage. We further believe the Bible defines marriage as a covenant-union between one man and one woman.

ARTICLE 12. This Association may exclude from its body any minister who teaches heresy or any member Quarterly that countenances him in said teaching or that may be disloyal to the tenets of Faith as held by this Association and expressed in our Articles of Faith.

ARTICLE 13. All questions coming before this Association shall be determined by a majority vote, except exclusions of member Quarterlies which shall require two-thirds majority.

ARTICLE 14. All member churches present and voting shall be considered a quorum for the transaction of business for each session.

ARTICLE 15. Amendments to this Constitution may be made at any time by a majority vote of the members present.

ARTICLE 16. This Association may adjourn to meet with any church that is a regular member of it at any time it deems proper.

ARTICLE 17. This Association, having jurisdiction over all member Quarterlies within its bounds, shall discipline any member Quarterly which allows a member church to call a minister for a pastor who has been excluded by the Presbytery.

BOARDS

ARTICLE 1. All standing boards shall be composed of four (4) members, with the exception of: The Ministerial Benevolence Board which shall be composed of five (5) members; the Christian Education Board which shall be composed of seven (7) members; the Youth Camp Board which shall be composed of eleven (11) members; and the Executive Board which shall be composed as provided in Article 2 under BOARDS.

The personnel of each of the forgoing boards, exclusive of the Executive, Ministerial Benevolence and Youth Camp Boards shall be elected as follows: the first named for a period of one (1) year, the second named for a period of two (2) years, and the third named for a period of three (3) years. Succession of office thereafter shall be determined, as order requires. The Ministerial Benevolence Board members shall be elected each year for a five (5) year term. The eleven member Youth Camp Board shall be elected on a three (3) member, four (4) member, four (4) member rotation basis with each member being elected for a three (3) year term.

The moderator of the Cumberland Association is to communicate with the chairmen of the standing boards during the year to assure their operation throughout the year.
The standing boards are to be represented at the Quarterly Meetings to promote their work. The standing boards are to meet at least twice a year to handle board matters and plan future activities.

ARTICLE 2. The personnel of the Executive Board shall be composed of the Moderator, Assistant Moderator, Clerk, Assistant Clerk, Treasurer, and the Moderators of each Quarterly meeting.

ARTICLE 3. The Executive Board shall have the power to act in behalf of and for the Cumberland Association from one regular session to another, and shall have power to elect such officers as may be necessary for its own government, and to carry out the plans and undertakings of the Association. It shall be the duty of the Executive Board to make written reports of all its work to each annual session of the Association.

ARTICLE 4. The duties of the various standing boards shall be to plan a program and supervise its operation in their respective fields. They shall organize themselves and regulate their work as may become necessary and as may be found in harmony with the principles and tenets of the Association.

The Duties of the International Mission Board
To promote international missions in each of the quarterly meetings by planning events to help undergird

International Missions.

The Duties of the Ministerial Benevolence Board
1. Soliciting for funds from association churches in order to carry out its ministry;
2. Administering those funds in a responsible and economical manner;
3. Providing regular monthly support for those who qualify and have served the Lord well within the fellowship of the Cumberland Association churches;
4. Keeping our ministers and laymen informed of benefits available to them in the form of hospital and special purpose insurance and retirement benefits.

The Objectives of the Youth Camp Board
1. To provide a Christian camping experience for the youth of the churches that make up the Cumberland Association of Free Will Baptists;
2. To evangelize and seek to win each camper to the Lord Jesus Christ;
3. To stimulate Christian growth and maturity through Bible classes; Missionary and Christian service classes, Christian Counseling, and through the preaching of God's Word;
4. To provide healthful physical activities and recreation for each camper;
5. To provide for various social activities for enjoyment and relaxation;
6. To uphold standards of modesty in behavior and in dress for boys and girls; and
7. To serve as trustees of the campground.

RULES AND DECORUM
This Association shall be opened by singing and prayer. Only one person may speak at a time. All addresses made by the members shall be made to the moderator, and the person thus speaking shall strictly confine himself to the subject in debate. No speaker shall cast any personal reflection toward any member of this body who has spoken previously.
No person shall be allowed to speak more than two times on any one subject without the permission of a majority of the Association.
The speaker shall not be interrupted during his speech by anyone except the moderator unless he violates the rules of order.
No member shall speak longer than ten minutes at any time without permission from the moderator.
Any member who shall willfully and knowingly violate any of these rules shall be reported by the moderator and shall be subject to the censure of the Association.
Adopted in Council this Saturday before the Lord's Day in October 1867 as a standing decorum, though subject to revision by majority of members voting for revision.

Constitution and Government revised: October 17, 1957, October 15, 1964, October 14, 1965, October 16, 1968, October 16, 1969, October 16, 1975, October 14, 1976, February 16, 1978, October 12, 1983, October 17, 1984, October 16, 1985, October 15, 1986, October 14, 1987, October 8, 1991, October 12, 1993, October 11, 1994, October 12, 1996, October 17, 2009, October 17, 2015

CUMBERLAND ASSOCIATION PRESBYTERY MINUTES
OCTOBER 15, 2016

Meeting of the Presbytery of the Cumberland Association of Free Will Baptists October 15, 2016

Reverend Larry Hampton, moderator, called the meeting to order. He offered thanks to the ladies of the church for providing the meal and commended Reverend Danny Dwyer for the message he delivered during the meeting of the association. A reminder was given to turn in report forms in order to receive a certificate of good standing with the presbytery.

Reverend Hampton stated that the Presbytery Board wanted to be a help to those they served and were open to suggestions for ways that they might do so. He stated that the board would like to see some of the experienced pastors begin to partner with some of the younger pastors to aide one another in the ministry and that the board would be glad to help facilitate those relationships.

Reverend Hampton brought a suggestion from the board that a gift of $1000 be given to Reverend Randy Corn as recognition for his many years of service to the association and in response to his resignation due to health problems. Motion made and seconded. Question: Can individuals contribute additional funds to the gift? Answer: Yes. The motion carried.

Question: Is there an update regarding the status of Reverend Corn's health? Answer: Reverend Dwayne James provided an update and directed the members to Reverend Corn's blog for further information.

Question: Is Reverend Corn still serving as a pastor? Answer: No, he resigned from his church.

Reverend Hampton moved to the election of officers. A proposal from the Presbytery Board was presented regarding the officer positions in the instance that there were no other nominees: Reverend Larry Hampton to serve as Moderator, Reverend Dwayne James to serve as assistant Moderator, Reverend Craig Batts to serve as Clerk/Treasurer. This would involve the exchanging of current roles between Reverend James and Reverend Batts, who currently served as Clerk/Treasurer and Assistant Moderator respectively. The floor was opened for nominations. No additional nominations were presented. A motion was made to accept the proposal from the Presbytery Board. The motion was seconded and carried. Reverend Hampton opened the floor for any new business. None was presented.

Reverend Eddie Hodges presented a word of commendation to the Presbytery Board and the Christian Education Board of the Cumberland Association for their efforts in providing a seminar for Dr. Robert Picirilli to discuss his most recent book on discipleship.

Reverend Hampton introduced Reverend Craig Batts to deliver a message. Reverend Batts presented a message from 1 Peter 1:1-13, where he spoke of our hope for tomorrow, our inspiration from the past, and our strength for today. He reminded us that the Gospel is the message that our broken world is desperately searching for, a message of hope that there is a better way.

Reverend Dwayne James, Clerk/Treasurer, brought his reports. The minutes from the 2015 meeting were read and a motion was made, seconded, and carried to receive the report as read. The financial report was presented and a motion was made, seconded, and carried to receive the report.

Question: Are there reports from the quarterly associations? Reports were then sought from representatives of the quarterlies.

Northern Quarterly: no report.

Western Quarterly: The credentials of Reverend Brian Bishop were ratified.

South Central: no report.

Southern Quarterly:

Received these members via transfer of credentials:

Chris Compton – Progressive Association of Alabama
Mike Hollis – Pamlico Association of North Carolina
Judson Phenicie – Rend Lake District of Illinois
Chris Talbot – Palmer Association of North Carolina
Lazaro Riesgo Acosta – Free Will Baptist Convention of Cuba.
Terry Welch – Western Quarterly

Granted a letter of good standing to Larry Powell in transfer of his credentials to the Martin Association of Georgia.

Examined Christopher Davenport for ordination and recommended him to the Donelson Fellowship.

Examined Greg Tucker for ordination and recommended him to Cross Timbers FWB Church.

Motion, seconded, and carried to receive these reports as information.

The meeting was adjourned in prayer by Reverend Richard Atwood.

CUMBERLAND ASSOCIATION PRESBYTERY TREASURERS REPORT
OCTOBER 1, 2016 - SEPTEMBER 30, 2017

Initial Deposit (1/30/17):	$3616.50
Checks Ordered:	$71.01
Supplies (envelopes, labels)	$64.97
Postage	$63.70

Clerk/Treasurer Payment $275.00
Total Expenditures   **$ 474.68**
Deposits   **$ 635.00**
Current Balance   **$3,776.82**

Respectfully submitted,
Craig Batts
Clerk/Treasurer

Other Ministers in the Cumberland Association 2017

Northern Quarterly
Reverend Craig Beeche, Reverend Seldon Buck, Reverend Eric Cowart,   Rev David Dell, Reverend Don Dungan, Rev Jon Forrest, Reverend Terry Forrest, Reverend Bob Hamm, Reverend Bud Hill, Reverend Eddie Hodges, Reverend Roy Jensen, Reverend Jon Justice, Reverend Chad Kivette, Reverend John Lee, Reverend Larry Lee, Reverend Tom Malone,
Reverend David Milling, Reverend Mark Milling, Reverend Phillip Morgan,
Reverend Lloyd Plunkett, Reverend Barry Simpson, Reverend Frank Slaughter, Reverend Eric Thomsen, Reverend Neal Thomsen, and Reverend Don Worrell.

Southern Quarterly
Reverend Eugene Workman, Reverend Keith Burden, Reverend Ron Callaway, Reverend Jeff Caudill, Reverend Jerry Gibbs, Reverend Roy Harris, Reverend Tim Hutchinson, Reverend Steve Lytle, Reverend Robert E Picirilli, Reverend Billy Walker, Reverend LeRoy Forlines,

Reverend Harrold Harrison, Reverend Don McDonald, Reverend Eddie Payne, Reverend Glenn Poston, Reverend David Williford, Reverend Robert Woodard,
Reverend Steve Greenwood, Reverend Corey Hawkins, Reverend Curt Holland, Reverend Ron Hunter, Reverend Dean Jones, Reverend Doug Little, Reverend Mark McPeak,
Reverend Jeff Nichols, Reverend Aaron Pontious, Reverend Norman Richards, Reverend Don Robirds, Reverend Henry Van Kluyve, Reverend Ray Lewis, Reverend Steve Marlin,
Reverend Jeff Skiles, Reverend Terry Welch, Reverend Lazaro Riesgo,
Reverend Stanley Outlaw, Reverend Robert J. Morgan, Reverend Garnett Reid, and Reverend Walter Ed Gragg.

South Central Quarterly
Reverend Ed Fox, Reverend Phil Perry, Reverend Clarence Porter, and Reverend Robert Wells.

Western Quarterly
Reverend James Carrington, Reverend Joshua Clark, Reverend Keith Buchanan, Reverend Bob Baggett,

GUIDELINES FOR LICENSED MINISTERS IN THE CUMBERLAND ASSOCIATION

I. RULES PERTAINING TO THE LICENSED MINISTER

A. Qualifications for the Licensee

    1. He must be a member of a church, which belongs to the Cumberland Association.

    2. He must give evidence to his church that he is divinely called to preach, whereupon the local church is authorized to examine him for license. This examination should include the areas of the candidate's life, doctrine, reputation, and his convictions and abilities regarding the work of the ministry. His present and prospective educational and professional qualifications should also be considered. Upon completion of such an examination, the local church shall determine whether or not to grant license.

       Their ministerial license shall be valid for a period of one year, but is renewable annually.

    3. He must have his license renewed annually by said church and kept in force until ordination.

B. The Activities of the Licensee

    1. According to the general practices of Free Will Baptists, a licensed minister is urged to afford himself every opportunity to preach the Word. He is free to exercise all the privileges and responsibilities of an ordained minister with the exception of pastoring a church and officiating at the observances of the ordinances and weddings.

    2. The licensee should consider the years between his receiving license and being ordained as years of study and training in preparation for his calling.

C. His Relationship to the Presbytery

The clerk of the church should report the names of licensed ministers to the clerk of the Presbytery who will forward a copy of these guidelines to each licensee. Licensed ministers will be eligible to hold associate membership in the Presbytery.

II. SUGGESTIONS FOR PREPARATION FOR ORDINATION

    A. Attend Free Will Baptist Bible College if possible.
    B. Seek counsel of an experienced pastor or pastors.
    C. Make as thorough a study as possible of the following:
        1. The Holy Bible
        2. Systematic Theology
        3. Homiletics
        4. Pastoral Theology and Church Administration
        5. Evangelism
        6. Church History (especially F.W.B. history)

III. A SUGGESTED SCHEDULE OF WORK LEADING TO ORDINATION

As soon as licensee feels that he is qualified to become a candidate for ordination, he should request a list of study questions from the Examining Committee of the Presbytery. We would strongly encourage him to proceed with his examination before entering a call to a church.

At least two months before the Examining Committee meets, he should secure the examination. He should make five copies of the completed examination (one for each member of the Committee), and send them to the Examining Committee no later than two weeks before its meeting.

Alternate: The Candidate will be given a written

examination based on some of the study questions in the presence of one or more of the Committee members.

The Candidate is required to pass an oral examination administered by the Committee.

The Committee will report to the candidate on whether he passed or what area he may need additional study.

When the approved candidate has passed the examination and has received a call to a church or is engaged in some other form of Christian service that would justify his being ordained, the Committee will recommend his ordination to the Presbytery. This recommendation will usually be made only after the candidate has been licensed for one year.

CONSTITUTION OF THE PRESBYTERY OF THE CUMBERLAND ASSOCIATION OF FREE WILL BAPTISTS

ARTICLE I: Name

This organization shall be known as the Presbytery of the Cumberland Association of Free Will Baptists of Tennessee.

ARTICLE II: Purpose

The purpose of this Presbytery shall be to promote fellowship, issue cards of good standing, provide opportunities for continuing education (such as seminars and retreats), and discipline its members.

ARTICLE III: Membership

The membership of this Presbytery shall consist of all ordained ministers and deacons holding cards of good standing in the Presbytery. This Presbytery may invite visiting ministers and deacons to sit in council with it in any assembly thereof. Licensed ministers in good standing with a member church of this Association are associate members of the Presbytery with no voting privileges.

ARTICLE IV: Officers

The officers of this Presbytery shall be a moderator, assistant moderator, clerk, and treasurer, who shall be elected annually and shall serve until their successors are elected.

ARTICLE V: Meetings

This Presbytery shall hold annual sessions at the close of the first day's session of the Cumberland Association. Called sessions may be held at the call of the moderator, his assistant, or any five members of said Presbytery who deems it necessary, upon written notice to the membership. Eleven members shall constitute a quorum.

ARTICLE VI: Committees

The discipline committee shall consist of the moderator, clerk, chairman, or his representative from each of the Quarterly examination committees. Other committees, as they are needed, may be appointed by the moderator.

ARTICLE VII: Amendments

This constitution may be amended at any regular meeting of the Presbytery by a two-thirds majority vote of the members present.

BY-LAWS

ARTICLE I: Ordination And Ratification

This Presbytery shall have the responsibility to establish guideline relating to the ordination of applicants to the Gospel Ministry and ratification of the credentials of ordained ministers transferring to the Cumberland Presbytery.

ARTICLE II: Cards Of Standing

This Presbytery shall issue annually cards of good standing to ministers upon the presentation of a report, in person (in case of sickness or some other legitimate reason letters may be accepted). Cards of good standing shall be issued annually to deacons upon the presentation of a letter of recommendation from their local churches. A donation of $5 per deacon is requested.

Any minister or deacon failing to hold a card of good standing shall not have a voice in this Presbytery. Any minister having lost his card of good standing may be reinstated in this Presbytery upon the presentation of his report and who manifests a sincere interest in the work of the Lord.

Ministers who have retired or who have reached the age of retirement and have continued to manifest a sincere interest in the work of the Lord may be issued a lifetime card of good standing which they may hold as long as they hold membership in this Presbytery or as long as their conduct is unquestionable.

Ministers who are members of churches in the Cumberland

Association who do not have cards of good standing do not have the approval of this body to present themselves in other Free Will Baptist meetings as a Free Will Baptist minister in good standing.

ARTICLE III: Discipline

The Presbytery shall have the power to try and withdraw fellowship from any member upon evidence of guilt of unchristian conduct, or who is teaching or preaching heresy or who has proven to be disloyal to the tenets of faith as expressed in the Treatise of the National Association of Free Will Baptists, as held by the Cumberland Association of Free Will Baptists of Tennessee.

ARTICLE IV: Donations

Each member of this Presbytery shall be asked to donate $5 annually upon the presentation of his report. This fund is to be used for acquiring necessary equipment, the printing of such materials as cards of good standing, constitution and by-laws, stationary, minutes of meetings and for defraying of necessary traveling and mailing expenses, and other needs authorized by the Presbytery.

ARTICLE V: Amendments

These by-laws may be amended at any regular meeting of this Presbytery by a two-thirds majority vote of members present.

>   Amended October 5, 1969
>   Amended October 14, 1980
>   Amended October 15, 1985

BY-LAWS OF CUMBERLAND YOUTH CAMP, INC.

ARTICLE I: Purposes and Powers

The purpose for which this corporation, hereinafter called the "Camp", is formed, and the powers it may exercise are those set forth in the Charter of Incorporation of the Camp.

ARTICLE II: Directors and Officers

Section 1. Number and qualifications of the directors. The business of the Camp shall be controlled by a board of eleven directors. No person shall be eligible for the office of director unless such a person is a member is good standing of a church within the Cumberland Association of Free Will Baptists.

Section 2. Election of directors. At the first annual meeting of the directors of the camp, directors shall be elected to succeed the incorporation directors. Three directors shall be elected for one year, three directors for two years, and three directors for three years, and thereafter, each director shall be elected for three years.

Section 3. Election of officers. The Board of Directors shall meet within 10 days after the first election and within 10 days after each annual election and shall elect by ballot a president, vice-president, secretary and treasurer (or secretary/treasurer), each of whom shall hold office until the election and qualification of his successor unless earlier removed by death, resignation, or for cause.

Section 4. Vacancies. Whenever a vacancy occurs in the Board of Directors, other than from the expiration of a term of office, the remaining directors shall appoint a member to fill the vacancy until the next regular meeting of the members.

Section 5. Special meetings. A special meeting of the Board of Directors shall be held whenever called by the President or by a majority of the directors. Any and all business may be transacted at a special meeting. Each call for a special meeting shall be in writing, signed by the person or persons making the same, addressed and delivered to the Secretary, and shall state the time and place of such meeting, and the matters to be acted upon.

Section 6. Notices of Board meetings. Notice of the regular or special meetings of directors shall be mailed to each director at least three (3) days prior to the time of such meeting, or notice may be telephoned to each director at least twenty-four (24) hours prior to the time of such meeting.

Section 7. Quorum. A majority of the Board of Directors shall constitute a quorum at any meeting of the Board.

ARTICLE III: Duties of Directors

Section 1. Management of business. The Board of Directors shall have general supervision and control of the business and the affairs of the Camp and shall make all rules and regulations not inconsistent with law or with these by-laws for the management of the business and the guidance of the members, officers, employees and agents of the Camp.

Section 2. Depository. The Board of Directors shall have the power to select one or more banks to act as depositories of the funds of the Camp and to determine the manner of receiving, depositing, and disbursing the funds of the Camp and the form of checks and the person or persons by whom same shall be signed, with the power to change, such banks and the person or persons signing such checks and the form thereof at will.

ARTICLE IV: Executive Committee

Section 1. Powers and duties. The Board of Directors may in its discretion appoint from its own membership an Executive Committee consisting of the President and two other members determine their tenure of office and their powers and duties. The Executive Committee shall have such powers as may, from time to time, be prescribed by the Board of Directors and these duties and powers may be all of the duties and powers of the said Board of Directors, subject to the general direction, approval, and control of the Board of Directors. Copies of the minutes of any meeting of the Executive Committee shall be mailed to all directors with seven (7) days following such meeting.

ARTICLE V: Duties of Officers

Section 1. Duties of President. The President shall (1) preside over all meetings of the Camp and of the Board of Directors, (2) call special meetings of the Board of Directors, (3) perform all acts and duties usually performed by an executive and presiding officer, and (4) sign such papers of the Camp as he may be authorized or directed to sign by the Board of Directors; provided, however, that the Board of Directors may authorize any person to sign any or all checks, contracts, and other duties as may be prescribed by the Board of Directors. Subject to the approval of the Board of Directors, the President shall employ, supervise, and dismiss all agents and employees of the Camp.

Section 2. Duties of the Vice-President. In the absence or disability of the President, the Vice-President shall perform the duties of the President; provided, however, that in case of death, resignation, or disability of the President, the Board of Directors may declare the office vacant and elect his successor.

Section 3. Duties of Secretary. The Secretary shall keep a complete record of all meetings of the Camp and of the Board of Directors and shall have general charge and supervision of the books and records of the Camp. He shall sign all contracts with the President and such other papers pertaining to the Camp as he may be authorized or directed to sign by the Board of Directors. He shall act as Secretary of the Executive Committee. He shall make all reports required by law and shall perform such other duties as may be required of him by the Camp or the Board of Directors. Upon the election of his successor, the Secretary shall turn over to him all books and other property belonging to the Camp that he may have in his possession. In general, under the direction of the Board of Directors, the Secretary shall be required to maintain his records and accounts in such a manner that the true and correct condition of the business may be ascertained therefrom at any time. He shall carefully preserve all books, documents, correspondence and records of whatever kind pertaining to the business which may come into his possession.

Section 4. Treasurer. The Treasurer shall perform such duties with respect to the finances of the Camp as may be prescribed by the Board of Directors.

ARTICLE VI: Operating Funds

Expense allocation. From the receipts of the Camp there shall be deducted the actual costs and expenses of operations, including wages, salaries, equipment, materials, or supplies, taxes, bonds and insurance, interest, repairs, depreciation, and any other costs or expenses of the Camp, and any balance shall be retained in a reserve for contingencies.

ARTICLE VII: Amendments

These By-Laws may be altered or amended at any regular meeting of the Board of Directors or at any special meeting of the members if notice of the character or the amendment(s) proposed has been given in the notice of the meeting, by the affirmative vote of a majority or more of the members present or voting by mail.

---

[i] Stanley J. Folmsbee, Robert E. Corlew, and Enoch L. Mitchell, *History of*
[ii] Harriette Simpson Arnow, *Seedtime on the Cumberland* (New York: Macmillan, 1960), 232.

[iii] Ibid., 217, 219.
[iv] See William F. Davidson's discussion of this topic in *The Free Will Baptists in History* (Nashville: Randall House Publications, 2001), 116.
[v] Roger Finke and Rodney Stark, *The Churching of America, 1776-2005: Winners and Loser in Our Religious Economy* (New Brunswick, NJ: Rutgers University Press, 2005), 59.

[vi] Robert E. Picirilli, *Little Known Chapters in Free Will Baptist History* (Nashville: Randall House, 2015), 37. It seems that Drake was one of the early settlers that arrived with the Heaton party. See Arnow, 219, 251.
[vii] Finke and Starke, 86.
[viii] Ibid., 101.

[ix] Albert J. Raboteau, *Slave Religion: The "Invisible Institution" in the Antebellum South* (1978; updated New York: Oxford University Press, 2004), 137. See also Christine Leigh Heyrman, *Southern Cross: The Beginnings of the Bible Belt* (Chapel Hill: University of North Carolina Press, 1997),67-69.

[x] Finke and Starke, 105.

[xi] It is very difficult to say exactly how many black people were included in Heatons record. The sparse nature of Heaton's notes is exacerbated by the fact that he used only first names for black people. Therefore, it is possible that there are as many as nineteen black people included in Heaton's record.

[xii] Heyrman, 46-48.

[xiii] For the names of Heaton's slaves see Picirilli, 35-36. It should be noted that the Jenny listed in Heaton's ministerial record may not refer to his slave at all, but to another woman.

[xiv] Picirilli, 40-42.

[xv] Ibid., 44. The spelling of the Nolin Association varies. I have chosen to follow Picirilli's spelling for the sake of consistency.

[xvi] *Minutes of the Nolynn Association of Separate Baptists, 1821* in *Minutes of the Nolynn Association of Separate Baptists, 1819-1884* transcribed by Charles E. Jordan Sr. (Executive Committee of the Nolynn Association, 1999), 9; accessed July 28, 2018, http://www.separatebaptist.org/downloads/nolynn/NolynnMinutes1819-1884.pdf.

[xvii] Picirilli, 52.

[xviii] *Minutes of the Nolynn Association of Separate Baptists, 1827* in *Minutes of the Nolynn Association of Separate Baptists, 1819-1884* transcribed by Charles E. Jordan Sr. (Executive Committee of the Nolynn Association, 1999), 39; accessed July 28, 2018, http://www.separatebaptist.org/downloads/nolynn/NolynnMinutes1819-1884.pdf.

[xix] *Minutes of the Nolynn Association of Separate Baptists, 1826* in *Minutes of the Nolynn Association of Separate Baptists, 1819-1884* transcribed by Charles E. Jordan Sr. (Executive Committee of the Nolynn Association, 1999), 35-36; accessed July 28, 2018, http://www.separatebaptist.org/downloads/nolynn/NolynnMinutes1819-1884.pdf.

[xx] *Minutes of the Nolynn Association of Separate Baptists, 1827* in *Minutes of the Nolynn Association of Separate Baptists, 1819-1884*, 39.

[xxi] *Minutes of the Nolynn Association of Separate Baptists, 1828* in *Minutes of the Nolynn Association of Separate Baptists, 1819-1884* transcribed by Charles E. Jordan Sr. (Executive Committee of the Nolynn Association, 1999), 46-47; accessed July 28, 2018, http://www.separatebaptist.org/downloads/nolynn/NolynnMinutes1819-1884.pdf.

[xxii] G. V. Frey, "The Gower Family and Historical Data of the Cumberland Association of Free Will Baptists" in *Minutes of the Cumberland Association of Freewill Christian Baptists, 1911* (Nashville: Executive Committee of the Cumberland Association, 1911), 27. Frey's short history of the Gower family is somewhat problematic, because it contains some factual inaccuracies, some of which he picked up from another source. However, such minor problems should not discredit Frey's account completely, especially in regards to larger points of historical development.

[xxiii] Arnow, 269, note 81.

[xxiv] John B. McFerrin, *History of Methodism in Tennessee,* vol. 1, *From the Year 1783 to the Year 1804* (Nashville: Publishing House of the M. E. Church, South, 1888), 379-380.

[xxv] The information regarding Gower's first marriage relies on genealogical research, which is very difficult to verify and can be unreliable at times. However, the same genealogical work confirmed my suspicion that Gower's second wife was the Lucindy Page listed in Heaton's journal. This information was accessed August 2, 2018, https://www.familycentral.net/index/pedigree.cfm?ref1=2017:68.

[xxvi] It is also possible that Gower had been raised a Methodist and simply chose to adopt believer's baptism.

[xxvii] Frey, 29. For education levels of Baptist ministers during the early nineteenth century see Finke and Starke, 77-79.

[xxviii] Ibid.

[xxix] Picirilli, 58-59.

[xxx] Ibid., 62-63.

[xxxi] Ibid., 60.

[xxxii] Ibid.

[xxxiii] Good Spring may or may not be the predecessor of the current Good Springs Free Will Baptist Church, which has been reconstituted several times.

[xxxiv] For more information on the multiple familial connections between Head and Gower see Phillip T. Morgan's *Heads Free Will Baptist Church:*

A Rich Heritage; A Bright Future (Cedar Hill, TN: Heads Free Will Baptist Church, 2015), 6, 8.

[xxxv] Joseph H. Borum, *Biographical Sketches of Tennessee Baptist Ministers* (1880; repr., Lafayette, TN: Church History Research and Archives, 1976), 247.

[xxxvi] The 1850 Census records his title as Reverend, but there is no supporting evidence in this regard.

[xxxvii] Finke and Stark, 73.

[xxxviii] Picirilli, 65.

[xxxix] Ibid., 61-62, 66-67.

[xl] *Minutes of the Cumberland Association of Separate Baptists, 1843* (Executive Committee of the Cumberland Association, 1843), 2.

[xli] Finke and Starke, 77.

[xlii] Frey, 29.

[xliii] Mary Ruth Wisehart, *Sparks into Flame: A History of the Woman's National Auxiliary Convention of the National Association of Free Will Baptists, 1935-1985* (Nashville: Woman's National Auxiliary Convention, 1985), 17.

[xliv] Ibid., 18.

[xlv] Ibid.

[xlvi] Ibid., 61.

[xlvii] Mary Ann Welch, "The Together Way" in Wisehart, *Sparks into Flame*, 20.

[xlviii] *Minutes of the Cumberland Association of Freewill Christian Baptists, 1919* ([Nashville, TN] : Executive Committee of the Cumberland Association, 1919), 9, 10.

[xlix] Ibid., 9.

[l] *Minutes of the Cumberland Association of Freewill Baptists, 1921* ([Clarksville], TN: Executive Committee of the Cumberland Association, 1921), 14.

[li] Ibid.

[lii] *Minutes of the State Convention of Ladies Aid Societies of the Freewill Baptists of Tennessee, 1928* (Ashland City, TN: Executive Committee of the Cumberland District Ladies Aid, 1928), 13-14.

[liii] *Minutes of the State Convention of Ladies Aid Societies of the Freewill Baptists of Tennessee, 1925* (Ayden, NC: Executive Committee of the Cumberland District Ladies Aid, 1925), 8.

[liv] *Minutes of the Cumberland Association of Freewill Baptists, 1921*, 14.

[lv] *Minutes of the Cumberland Association of Freewill Baptists, 1922* (Clarksville, TN: Executive Committee of the Cumberland Association, 1922), 10.
[lvi] Ibid.
[lvii] Ibid.
[lviii] *Minutes of the Ladies' Aid Convention, 1931* in *Minutes of the Union Free Will Baptist Association, 1931* (Hawkins County, TN: Executive Committee of the Union Association, 1931), 15.
[lix] *Minutes of the General Conference of the Original Free Will Baptist of the United States, 1929* (Ayden, NC: Executive Committee of the General Conference, 1929), 8.
[lx] *Minutes of the General Conference of the Original Free Will Baptist of the United States, 1931* (Ayden, NC: Executive Committee of the General Conference, 1931), 15.
[lxi] Wisehart, 63.
[lxii] *Minutes of the General Conference of the Original Free Will Baptist of the United States, 1931*, 15.
[lxiii] *Minutes of the General Conference of the Original Free Will Baptist of the United States, 1930* (Ayden, NC: Executive Committee of the General Conference, 1930), 6.
[lxiv] *Minutes of the General Conference of the Original Free Will Baptist of the United States, 1929*, 8.
[lxv] *Minutes of the General Conference of the Original Free Will Baptist of the United States, 1933* (Ayden, NC: Executive Committee of the General Conference, 1933), 20.
[lxvi] Agnes Frazier interview by Pat Thomas (Ashland City, TN: June 11, 1982); available in the Welch College Archive.
[lxvii] Wisehart, *Sparks to Flame*, 51.
[lxviii] *Minutes of the Convention of Ladies Aid Societies of Free Will Baptists of Cumberland Association, of Tennessee, 1929* ([Nashville]: Executive Committee of the Cumberland District Ladies Aid, 1929), 4.
[lxix] Ibid.
[lxx] Obituary in *Tennesseean* (April 25, 1964), 16.
[lxxi] *Minutes of the General Conference of the Original Free Will Baptist of the United States, 1931*, 16; and *Minutes of the General Conference of the Original Free Will Baptist of the United States, 1934* (Ayden, NC: Executive Committee of the General Conference, 1934), 17.

[lxxii] *Minutes of the Cumberland Association of Freewill Baptists, 1920* (Clarksville, TN: Executive Committee of the Cumberland Association, 1920), 10.
[lxxiii] *Minutes of the Cumberland Association of Freewill Baptists, 1921*, 14.
[lxxiv] Ibid.
[lxxv] *Minutes of the State Convention of Ladies Aid Societies of the Freewill Baptists of Tennessee, 1926* (Ayden, NC: Executive Committee of the Cumberland District Ladies Aid, 1926), 10.
[lxxvi] *Minutes of the Organizational Meeting of the Tennessee State Association of Free Will Baptists, 1938* (typewritten transcript by Robert E. Picirilli, 1971), [1].
[lxxvii] Ibid., [6].
[lxxviii] Ibid., [5].
[lxxix] *Minutes of the State Convention of Ladies Aid Societies of the Freewill Baptists of Tennessee, 1928* (Ashland City, TN: Executive Committee of the Cumberland District Ladies Aid, 1928), 6.
[lxxx] Ibid.
[lxxxi] *Minutes of the General Conference of the Original Free Will Baptist of the United States, 1928* (Ayden, NC: Executive Committee of the General Conference, 1928), 8.
[lxxxii] *Minutes of the General Conference of the Original Free Will Baptist of the United States, 1925* (Ayden, NC: Executive Committee of the General Conference, 1925), 8.
[lxxxiii] Wisehart, 63.
[lxxxiv] Ibid., 33.
[lxxxv] Ibid., 27.
[lxxxvi] Ibid.
[lxxxvii] Ibid., 63.
[lxxxviii] Agnes B. Frazier, letter to Lorene Miley, June 18, 1956 ("WNAC Materials" in BL-7 (cont.) of the Historical Collection).
[lxxxix] Wisehart, 64.
[xc] *Minutes of the Organizing Meeting of the National Auxiliary Convention, June 11-14, 1935* ("WNAC Materials" in BL-7 (cont.) of the Historical Collection).
[xci] Wisehart, 38.

www.ingramcontent.com/pod-product-compliance
Lightning Source LLC
Chambersburg PA
CBHW022356040426
42450CB00005B/207